Jules Fallon

Sewing for the Soul

Simple sewing patterns
and recipes to lift the spirits

DAVID & CHARLES

www.davidandcharles.com

Contents

6   Introduction

8   Tools and Equipment

10 Fabrics and Haberdashery

12 How to Use This Book

14 SPRING

16 Shirt Dress

24 Woven Tee

30 Embroidered Tee

34 Chocolate Orange Cake
    & Homemade Mocha Latte

38 SUMMER

40 Palazzo Pants

48 Shirred Summer Top

54 Cami and Shorts

60 Lemon Drizzle Cake
    & Homemade Elderflower Cordial

64 AUTUMN

66 Oversized Shirt

74 Classic T-shirt

80 Reloved Blanket

84 Spiced Sugar Crust Apple Cake
    & Hot Cider Nog

88 WINTER

90 Winter Coat

98 Drawstring Trousers

104 Christmas Stocking

108 Rich Fruit Cake with Hidden Surprises
     & Mulled Wine

112 General Sewing Techniques

124 Templates

126 About the Author

126 Acknowledgements

127 Index

Introduction

The concept for this book had been at the back of my mind for a while, but but when I found myself, like others, isolated for a long period recently it highlighted to me just how important it is to take time out for creativity.

The physical act of making something, using your hands and mind to connect together to create a 'thing', removes you from the mundane and sometimes painful situations of the everyday. More and more, we are seeking the solace of creativity to help us deal with situations we might not want to be in and we are finding the deep and lasting joy of creating.

I find this happening in every workshop and retreat that I teach. The satisfaction and achievement that people are able to feel is evident in their faces and it warms my heart to know that I have shared some of what I feel with others.

I find that sewing helps me retain my sense of equilibrium. It helps me concentrate and plan, as I have to be aware of what I need for each project I undertake, and focusing on each process in turn increases my patience as I have to wait for the finished item to reveal itself. I have also learnt to control my frustrations, as a quiet mind makes for better sewing, and I've made friends with my un-picker. Sewing really does feed my soul.

I have structured this book around the seasons, as I am becoming more and more aware of how the way I feel is linked to the world around me and have started to delight in the changes I see throughout the year. Each chapter or season in the book has a 'slow-sew' project, something a little bit more meaty that you can get your teeth into, that may take several days to complete; a 'quick-sew' project that you should be able to complete in a couple of afternoons and is a good one for getting your sewing mojo up and running; and a re-purposing project. I love the idea of transforming something you love that has seen better days into something new that you can make use of again.

There are a couple of recipes for each season that I hope you'll enjoy, too. We always invite people in for a cuppa and a piece of cake in all our workshops. You can put the world to rights over a coffee and cake and make a whole host of new friends, too. Cake really is soul food.

Each season of the year has its own joys and challenges — and if you can relish and overcome those challenges through finding solace in sewing, I will feel I have passed just a bit of my own joy on to you.

Happy sewing!

Jules x

Tools and Equipment

You don't need a huge amount of equipment to get started, but a few quality items will make your sewing far more pleasurable. This is what I recommend as a basic sewing kit; once you have these items, you can add others on your wish list as a gift to yourself.

SEWING MACHINE / OVERLOCKER
It doesn't matter how old your sewing machine is: as long as you can comfortably sew forwards and backwards, you can make clothes and other projects, too. Just make sure you look after your machine by regularly removing excess lint and threads from the mechanism.

There are ways of neatening seams to prevent them from fraying and keep them strong, but an overlocker (serger) will make your life so much easier and enable you to achieve a neat and professional finish. You will also be able to work with jersey and knit fabrics much more easily and quickly.

SEWING MACHINE NEEDLES
Keep a selection, as one will always break when you least expect it. Universal needles are usually size 80, but I prefer to have a range of sizes to correspond with the fabrics I want to use. Use a size 70 for lightweight fabrics and size 90 for denim and heavyweight fabrics. You can also use specialty needles for particular jobs. Topstitching needles, jersey or stretch needles, and twin needles are useful to have close to hand.

DRESSMAKING SHEARS
A quality pair of dressmaking shears that will happily slice through multiple layers of fabric is a must. Traditional stainless-steel shears are wonderful, as you can keep them nice and sharp, but the more modern micro-serrated ones are a great alternative.

EMBROIDERY OR STUDIO SCISSORS
A smaller pair of scissors will help you clip into those tight corners and is handy for trimming off loose threads.

PAPER SCISSORS
Obviously, you would never dream of using either of the above to cut paper – heaven forbid! So a regular pair of household scissors is great for cutting patterns and other non-fabric items.

ROTARY CUTTER AND SELF-HEALING MAT
Personally I prefer to cut with a good pair of shears. However, there are occasions when a rotary cutter makes life quicker and easier, particularly when you're cutting jersey or knit fabrics or cutting straight lines to make bias binding. It's always best to use a self-healing cutting mat underneath to prevent doing serious damage to your dining-room table.

TAPE MEASURE
This is an essential item and one I have permanently around my neck. The flexibility of a good tape measure will allow you to measure curves as well. Try and find a good-quality one, as cheaper versions can stretch over time, compromising your accuracy.

PINS
Long, stainless-steel dressmaker's pins are ideal. They will last longer and are fine enough to use for lightweight fabrics. You may find glass-headed pins easier to see and they will not melt under the heat of the iron.

PIN CUSHION
You definitely need somewhere to store your pins and everyone has their preference, whether it's a traditional tomato-shaped pincushion with strawberry sharpener, a wrist pincushion to carry your pins with you or just a plain old saucer. Just make sure your pins are within easy reach.

TAILOR'S CHALK AND MARKER PENS
I always have both, as each has its merits depending on the fabric you are marking. I prefer a traditional triangle of chalk, as you can sharpen the edges to keep it nice and accurate. Water-soluble marker pens are incredibly useful, too – but do test them on a scrap of fabric first, to make sure the marks will wash out.

SEAM RIPPER
Mine is never far from my reach, as even after all these years of sewing I still use it on a regular basis. There are some beautiful ones out there that have replaceable blades. Otherwise have a couple in your sewing box, as they can blunt very quickly.

IRON AND IRONING BOARD
An iron with a bit of weight behind it is worth its weight in gold, as proper pressing throughout the sewing process will make a huge difference to the quality of your finished project.

Make sure the ironing board you're using is the right height for you to work on and pretty sturdy, as they can take a lot of pressure sometimes. It is also important to ensure that it has plenty of padding. An ironing board with little or no padding will not support your fabric as you press it and could leave unpleasant marks. It is very easy to make your own replacement cover if you need one.

PRESSING CLOTH

This is an essential item. It doesn't have to be anything fancy, as long as it can diffuse the heat from the iron and protect the surface of the fabric you are working on; a spare bit of calico is fine. However, if you want to treat yourself, silk organza is the perfect choice for a pressing cloth.

TAILOR'S HAM

This isn't necessarily an essential item, but it is an incredibly useful one. A tailor's ham is a ham-shaped cushion stuffed tight with sawdust. One side is usually a woollen fabric to grip, the other a smooth calico to slide. They are just the ticket for helping to press three-dimensional shapes such as sleeve heads or necklines. You can make your own very easily or just use a rolled-up towel.

Fabrics and Haberdashery

The fabrics used for the projects in this book are all made from natural fibres. This is my personal preference; you can obviously choose the fabrics that you feel most comfortable with. That's one of the wonderful things about making your own clothes – you make what makes you happy.

WOVEN FABRICS

Anyone who knows me will know that linen is my absolute favourite. It's a wonder fabric! It keeps you cool in the summer and warm in the winter, and I could bore you endlessly with its fascinating history. I know some people are not keen on it because of the way it creases, but these days I would rather rock the crumpled look than the corporate look.

Cotton is another fibre that's heavily featured in this book because of its texture and breathability. But although there's little to beat the smell and feel of freshly laundered cotton left to dry in the sunshine, the lack of sustainability concerns me. This is why I try and look for beautiful fabrics that have had a previous life, such as embroidered tablecloths or retro patterned curtains. If you're careful with your cutting, there will often be enough usable fabric to create something new and wonderful.

Wool is a more sustainable fabric and one I love for wrapping yourself up in, either as a super-soft blanket or a protective winter coat. It has the most amazing properties and is even naturally waterproof; you never see a sheep with an umbrella! So it is perfect for cold, damp autumnal days. It's a beautiful fabric to work with and almost has a life of its own as you can steam and mould it into shape to help get a better fit to your clothes.

Although it's considered to be 'man made', viscose is actually derived from cellulose or reconstituted wood pulp. However it requires extensive processing with various chemicals to turn it into the fibres that can be spun and woven into fabrics. It has beautiful draping qualities and, because it is chemically similar to cotton, it has the same breathable properties, making it ideal for lightweight summer garments. Modern viscose production is now seen as more sustainable because the factories creating it use a 'closed system', meaning that the liquids and chemicals used in the creation of viscose are recycled within the whole process and not just discarded as polluting waste. It also takes up colour extremely well, so it's great for highly coloured printed patterns on fabrics.

KNIT FABRICS

Knit or jersey fabrics should contain at least 3-5% elastane to help the fabric return back to its original shape after being worn or stretched. I much prefer the feel of natural fibres next to my skin, so I would always opt for an organic cotton jersey or one that contains a mix of linen and cotton. As a hollow fibre, linen has better wicking properties than cotton so it will help to wick away any sweat or perspiration, leaving you feeling lovely and fresh.

Knit fabrics need to be treated differently to woven fabrics when it comes to sewing them. To prevent holes and ladders appearing in knit fabrics, use a ballpoint needle in your sewing machine. This has a slightly blunted and rounded point, so it can push between the strands of yarn that make up the fabric, rather than piercing them.

Knits also need to be handled with care and require very gentle minimal pressing to flatten the seams. Because it is created from one strand of yarn there is a lot more flexibility in the fabric, which we want to make use of. However, this also means that it is not as robust as its woven counterpart. Try to hover the iron above the fabric and use steam to set the press rather than the weight of the iron itself.

HABERDASHERY

As you develop your sewing habit, you will find yourself collecting and acquiring all manner of haberdashery items. Some you will use regularly, while others will only be for specific tasks or projects.

I like to have a stash of lightweight interfacing. as it's the type I use most often. I save scraps and keep them zipped away in a large project bag.I also find myself snipping off buttons from discarded clothing. I string them together on a piece of butcher's twine and add them to the ever-increasing stash that I keep in an old biscuit tin.

Sewing thread is another category that will start to increase as you add new colours for the different projects you work on, although it is always worth having a stash of navy, white and grey, as they will go with almost everything. If you use an overlocker, it will usually require four threads. I generally get five so thatI can have both my sewing machine and overlocker threaded up in the same colour. Some people I know have developed a fondness for rainbow-coloured threads on their overlockers and just use that for everything. I think this is a fabulous idea as the insides of your garments will always be cheerfully colourful.

Zips are something else to consider having in your stash. I tend to go for zips that are longer than I think I might need, because it's easier than you might think to reduce a zip to the correct size. Most dress zips are made of nylon and concealed zips certainly are. The only zips used in the projects in this book are trouser ones, so you can use either metal or nylon and either type can be shortened to fit your project.

Elastic comes in different widths and is another stash staple. I always have a few metres of elastic 3–5cm (1–2in) wide for waistbands. Another useful width to have is 1cm (⅜in) wide elastic. This is perfect for threading though necklines and cuffs, as it will add to the elastication but will still be stable enough to keep its shape.

I am incredibly lucky to have my own fabric store, so I am really spoilt when it comes to choosing fabrics for my own sewing projects. But I always stroke and feel the fabrics before making my final decision – and if it makes me smile, then it goes in the basket.

How to Use this Book

THE PATTERNS

Full-size patterns are included separately for all the projects except the self-drafted ones. The garment patterns come in different sizes from UK 8–26 (US 4–22), with each size on the pattern sheets marked in a different style of line. Each project is printed in a different colour, so it will be easy to see which lines relate to which project.

To use the pattern sheets, you will need to trace off all the pattern pieces in your chosen size. You can use a highlighter pen to mark the lines you need to follow if that makes it easier. Trace the pattern pieces onto plain pattern paper, remembering to copy all the pattern information such as darts, notches and pleats, and to name the individual pattern pieces before you cut them out.

To make tracing easier, use a ruler wherever there is a straight line and draw curves as a series of dashed lines rather than trying to follow the curve with one continuous line.

Once you have cut out the paper pattern and laid it out on the fabric, transfer all the notches, dart and pleat lines and any other information onto the fabric (see General sewing techniques: Transferring pattern markings).

SIZING

The patterns in this book are casual and comfortable to wear, so a fair amount of ease is included. (Ease is basically the space between your body and the garment – so more ease means a more comfortable and relaxed fit.)

Whatever your usual high-street size is, double check the body measurements and finished garment measurements on each project, as that will give you a better guide as to which size to make.

Take your own body measurements by measuring around yourself with a tape measure at the bust, waist and hip. The bust measurement needs to be around the fullest part of your bust, the waist measurement on your natural waistline and the hips around the fullest part of your buttocks. Remember to keep the tape measure horizontal and parallel to the ground, making sure that it is snug but not tight.

Use the chart below to compare your body measurements to our individual sizes and select the one that most closely matches your own.

Garment Size																	
8		10		12		14		16		18		20		22		24		26	
Body Measurements (cm and inches)																	
	cm	inch	cm	inch	cm	inch	cm	inch	cm	inch	cm	inch	cm	inch	cm	inch	cm	inch	cm	inch
Bust	82	32⅜	86	34	90	35⅝	95	37½	100	39½	105	41⅞	110	43¼	115	45¼	120	47¼	125	49¼
Waist	68	26⅞	72	28½	76	30	81	32	86	34	91	36⅜	96	37¾	101	39¾	106	41¾	111	43¾
Hips	90	35⅝	94	37⅛	98	38¾	103	40⅝	108	42⅝	113	45	118	46½	123	48½	128	50½	133	52½

Tip

If you are using a patterned fabric, check to see if it has a directional print. If it does, make sure that all the pattern pieces are lying in the correct direction to avoid upside-down flowers etc.

LAY PLANS

Following the lay plans for each project will ensure that you get the best use from your fabric and that you have all the pattern pieces positioned correctly; make sure the grain lines on the pattern pieces are parallel to the selvedges unless instructed otherwise.

There will be a lay plan for each project and each size group, if required, as different-sized patterns may require a different way of laying them out. Follow the lay plan for the size you are making.

Most pieces are cut with the fabric doubled so that the selvedges are together. It doesn't matter if you have the right or the wrong sides together. This means you will be cutting a pair of matching pattern pieces. If the pattern pieces needs to be cut on the fold, make sure that the edge of the paper is right on the folded edge of the fabric.

Selvedges

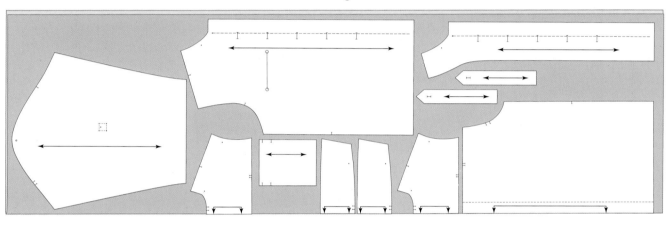

Fold

Lay out all the pattern pieces first to make sure they are going to fit correctly, then pin the pieces that are to be on the fold first before pinning the rest.

Sometimes patterns need to be cut in a single layer of fabric, as with the camisole and shorts patterns. This is because the pattern uses the bias grain of the fabric, which means that the pieces should be placed diagonally across the fabric rather than parallel to the selvedges.

Selvedge

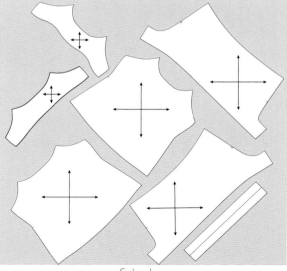

Selvedge

Spring

Shirt Dress

This slow-sew project is one to savour, as you can really go to town with all the detailing. I love topstitching, as you can see from the sample, and a plain fabric allows you to showcase some lovely topstitching detail in a contrasting colour of thread. However, the design works equally well in a print fabric that would not need much additional adornment.

The pockets, too, are an area where you can really make this dress your own. I've included back and breast patch pockets as well as pockets sewn into the side seam, but you could leave off the patch pockets – or even add more! – if you wish. For a really unique take, why not embellish the pockets with some simple embroidery? Just make sure that your decorative stitching doesn't extend into the pockets' seam allowances.

Buttons are the finishing touch and definitely worth taking time and care over, as they can make or break a garment. There's a wealth to choose from, from vintage buttons sourced from charity shops or antique stalls to up-to-the-minute fastenings that will give a cutting-edge look to a classic garment. As my old needlework teacher used to say, 'Buttons are like eyes: they are the windows into the soul of your sewing'.

Fabric Choices

This style of dress works best in something that has a little bit of substance to it, so linen or lightweight denim would be ideal. If you are more confident handling fabric, then a beautiful viscose rayon would be lovely to work with, too.

YOU WILL NEED

- 2.9m (3¼yd) main fabric, 140–150cm (55–60in) wide
- 1.2m (48in) lightweight iron-on interfacing
- 10 buttons, 1.5–2cm (⅝–¾in) in diameter
- Matching thread
- Contrasting topstitching thread (optional)
- Contrast bias binding (optional)
- Basic sewing kit (see Tools and Equipment)
- Topstitching needle
- Buttonhole foot

PATTERN INVENTORY

- A   Dress front – cut 2 in fabric
- B   Dress back – cut 2 in fabric
- C   Sleeve – cut 2 in fabric
- D   Collar – cut 2 in fabric
      and 1 on fold in interfacing
- E   Front facing – cut 2 in fabric
      and 2 in interfacing
- F   Back neck facing – cut 1 on fold in
      fabric and 1 on fold in interfacing
- G   In-seam pocket bag – cut 4 in fabric
- H   Back pocket – cut 2 in fabric
- I   Breast pocket – cut 2 in fabric
- J   Belt loops – cut 1 in fabric
- K   Belt – cut 1 in fabric

All seam allowances are 1.5cm (⅝in) unless otherwise stated.

FABRIC

INTERFACING

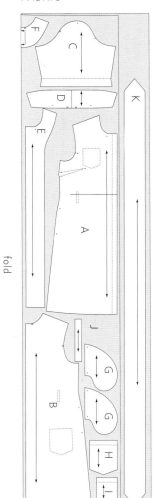

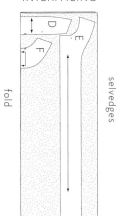

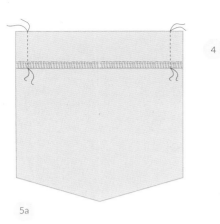

4

5a

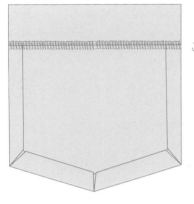

5b

6a

6b

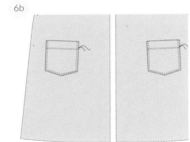

A LITTLE BIT OF PREP

1 Cut out the pattern pieces, following the lay plans (see General Sewing Techniques: Cutting out).

2 Transfer the pattern markings to your fabric (see General Sewing Techniques: Transferring pattern markings).

3 Apply interfacing to the upper collar and facing pieces (see General Sewing Techniques: Interfacing). Staystitch the necklines of the facing pieces (see General Sewing Techniques: Machine stitching). Staystitch the necklines on the dress front and back pieces too.

PATCH POCKETS

4 Neaten the top edges of the front and back patch pockets. Fold over the tops of the pockets along the foldline so that the right sides are together. Taking a 1cm (⅜in) seam allowance, sew across the short ends to create a facing. Turn the pocket facing right side out and winkle out the corners.

5 Press under the seam allowances around the sides of the pockets, mitring the corners (a). Topstitch across the bottom of the pocket facing to hold it in place (b) (see General Sewing Techniques: Machine stitching).

6 Place the patch pockets on the front of the dress along the placement line (a). Do the same with the back patch pockets (b). Topstitch around the side and bottom edges of each pocket to secure it in place.

DRESS

7   On the front dress, pinch out the bust darts and pin in place. Sew along the dart line from the edge to the point. Pivot at the point and sew back up into the dart. Press the dart up towards the armhole.

8   With right sides together, matching up the small dots, place the in-seam pocket bags on the dress front and back side seams. Sew with a 1cm (⅜in) seam allowance, then neaten the seam on the **dress back** sections only.

9   Press the pocket bags away from the dress and understitch the **dress front** pockets (see General Sewing Techniques: Machine stitching).

10 With right sides together, pin and sew the centre back seam. Neaten the seam allowances together and press to one side. If you wish, you can topstitch the seam from the right side for a bit of extra detail and decoration. Pin and sew the fronts to the back at the shoulder seams, then neaten and press the shoulder seams in the same way.

11 With right sides together, matching up the underarm point, the pocket bags and the hems, pin the front and back together at the side seams. Sew down the side seam on each side, pivoting at each small dot to sew around the pocket bags and then continuing down the rest of the side seam. Neaten the seam allowances together.

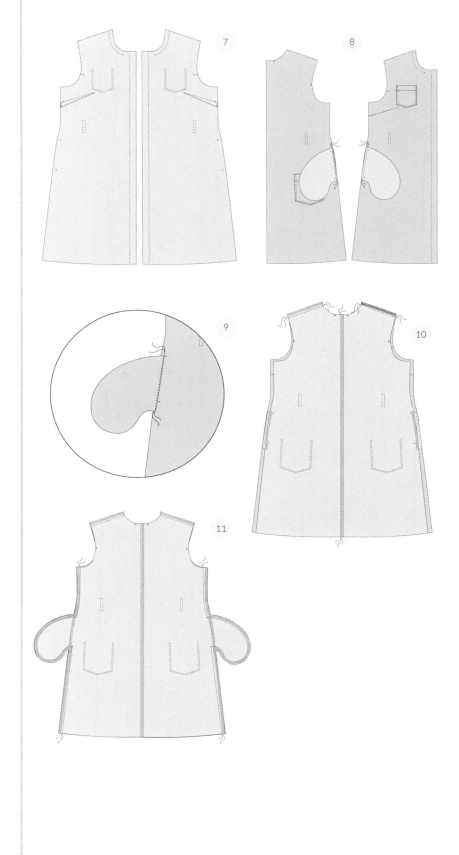

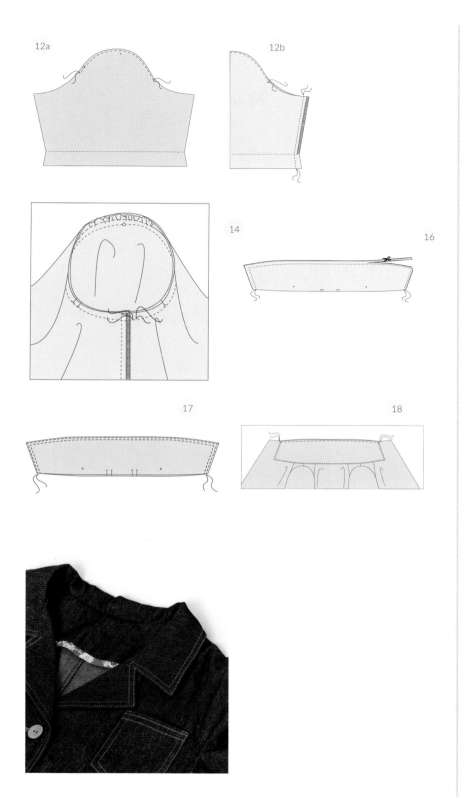

SLEEVES

12 Sew a row of easing stitches across the sleeve head between the notches (see General Sewing Techniques: Machine stitching)(a). With right sides together, sew the underarm seam(b). Neaten the seam allowances together from the armhole edge to the cuff foldline and press to one side.

13 Neaten the hem of the sleeve and press up 4cm (1½in) for the hem. Topstitch in place.

14 Matching up the underarm seam and side seam, single and double notches and the dot on the sleeve head with the shoulder seam, set the sleeve into the armhole. Ease the sleeve head to fit the armhole and pin in place. Sew around the armhole and neaten the seam.

COLLAR AND FACING

15 Trim 3mm (⅛in) from the outer edge and short sides of the under collar. This makes it roll under slightly and creates a much neater finish.

16 Place the upper and under collars right sides together. Ease the under collar out to fit the upper collar. Pin and sew along the outer edge and short sides. Trim the seam allowance down to 5mm (¼in) and carefully trim off the corners.

17 Turn the collar right side out and press it flat so that the seam is just on the edge. Topstitch the collar from the right side for a bit of extra detail and decoration.

18 With the under collar next to the dress, centre the collar on the back neckline. Match up the dots on the collar with the shoulder seams and make sure the collar sits on the large dots on the dress front. Machine baste in place.

19 Match up the shoulders of the back neck facing and the front facing pieces. Pin and sew across the shoulder seams. Press the seams open. Neaten the outer edge of the whole facing: you can either overlock or zigzag, as shown in the illustration, or use a contrast binding.

20 Neaten the hem of the dress.

21 Place the facing and dress right sides together, with the collar sandwiched in between. Match up all the key points and notches from the centre back neck along the neckline, around the lapel and down the front to the hem, and pin in place.

22 Sew across the facing at the hem, pivot and sew up the centre front, pivot at the point of the lapel and again at the collar. Make sure not to sew a stitch onto the collar itself before pivoting to sew around the neckline. Do the same in reverse to sew down the other side of the dress.

23 Carefully trim, layer and clip the seam allowances (see General Sewing Techniques: Reducing bulk).

24 Turn the facing and collar out to the right side. Roll the seam so that it sits right on the edge, then press carefully to set it in place. Topstitch along the facing and lapel to tie in with the topstitching on the collar. Press up the hem of the dress and topstitch around the hem.

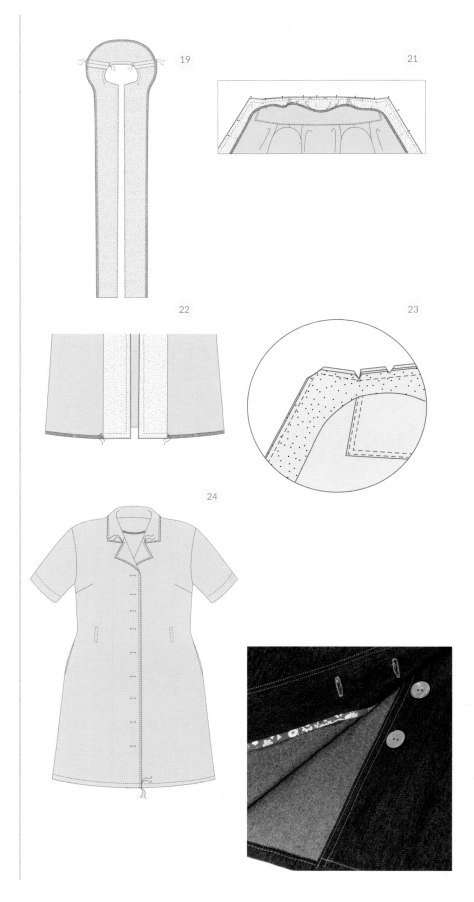

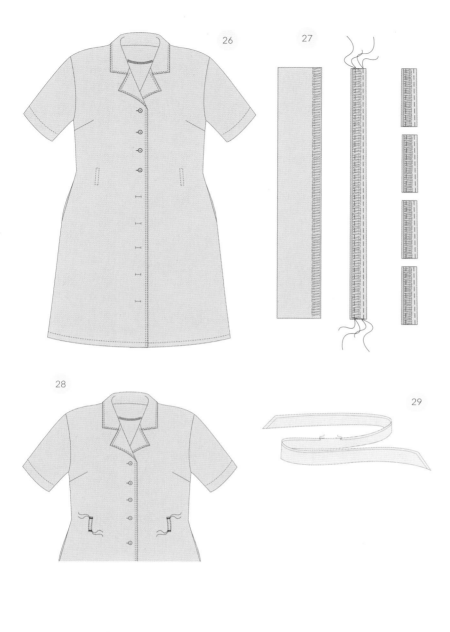

BUTTONHOLES AND BUTTONS

25 Using the pattern markings as a guide, transfer the buttonhole lines onto the right-hand side of the dress. Check they are in the correct place for you and adjust if necessary.

26 Sew the buttonholes the correct size for your buttons and carefully open them up (see General Sewing Techniques: Buttonholes and buttons). Lay out the dress and mark the button positions through the buttonholes along the centre front line. Sew on the buttons in the correct places.

BELT

27 Neaten one long edge of the belt loop piece, then fold it lengthways into thirds, with the neatened edge on the outside. Sew a double row of topstitching along the belt loop piece. Cut into four 8cm (3in) long pieces.

28 Press under 1cm (⅜in) on each short end of the individual belt loops. Pin in place over the belt loop markings and sew across the folded edges with a small zig-zag stitch to fix the belt loops to the dress.

29 Fold the belt in half lengthways, with the right sides together. Sew along the outer edge, leaving a gap of about 10cm (4in) in the middle and remembering to pivot at the corners. Turn the belt through to the right side and roll the seam to the edge. Press everything nice and flat. Topstitch along the belt for decoration and to close the gap in the seam.

Woven Tee

If you're new to sewing, or just want to make something that you can sew and wear the same day, this tee is just the thing. The simple shape makes it easy to sew and it can be made up in any lightweight woven fabric such as linen, cotton lawn or even a double gauze — all of which are easy to handle and perfect for stress-free sewing.

This is a pattern that you can draft straight from your own body measurements, making it totally unique to you. Once you have your pattern you can make as many as you choose, in whatever colour or fabric takes your fancy. It's incredibly versatile — the ultimate wardrobe staple. Pair it with jeans when you want to dress down, or with a flowing, calf-length skirt or smart trousers for a chic evening out.

Fabric Choices

Use any lightweight woven fabric such as linen, cotton lawn or even a double gauze.

DRAFTING THE PATTERN

If you are drafting your own pattern, there are a couple of things to remember!

- Always use a sharp pencil. It really makes a difference to the accuracy of your patterns.

- All lines that cross or meet at right angles really must be true right angles. I use Dot and Cross Pattern Paper to make sure of this, but you can use a sharp square edge instead.

You can make the neckline slightly smaller or larger, as you prefer, but use these measurements as a starting point.

1 Start by drawing a vertical line at the left-hand edge of your paper: this is the centre back/centre front line of the tee. Across the top of that line, draw a horizontal line; this is the shoulder line. Where the lines cross, mark this as **point 0**.

2 To find **point 1**, measure 11cm (4⅜in) across from 0. Drop a line vertically down from this point.

3 To find **point 2**, measure 14cm (5½in) down from 0. Measure from the Side neck, not the CF neck. From point 2, draw a line at right angles to the centre line so that it crosses the line down from point 1. This is the cradle for the front neckline.

4 To find **point 3**, with arms outstretched, measure from elbow crease to elbow crease across your chest, divide that measurement by 2 and mark that distance from 0 on the shoulder line. Drop a line vertically down from point 3, at right angles to the shoulder line.

5 Now measure and mark the following lines and points:

- Line 3–4: The measurement around your bicep.

- Line 0–5: The measurement from point 1 (the side of your neck) down to the finished length of the top.

- Line 5–6: A quarter of your hip measurement plus 3cm (1¼in).

- Point 7: Draw a line up from point 6 to meet a line coming horizontally across from point 4.

- Point 8: Measure the distance from point 7 to point 4 and draw a line the same length down from point 7.

- Point 9: Measure 7cm (2¾in) up from point 6.

- Point 10: Measure 4.5cm (1¾in) down from point 0. Draw a line at right angles from point 10 to the line down from point 1. This is the cradle for the back neckline.

6 For the **front pattern**, draw in the outline through points 1, 3, 4, 8, 9, 5 and 2. From 2–1, draw in a smooth curve that is almost a quarter circle. From 4–8, draw in a smooth curve that is almost a quarter circle. Curve the line from 9 to 5, ending the curve about 8cm (3⅛in) from point 5.

7 For the **back pattern**, draw in the outline through points 1, 3, 4, 8, 9, 5 and 10. Using a different colour of pencil, draw in a smooth curve from 10 to 1 with a slightly flat bottom to sit across the back neck. Then follow the shape for the front.

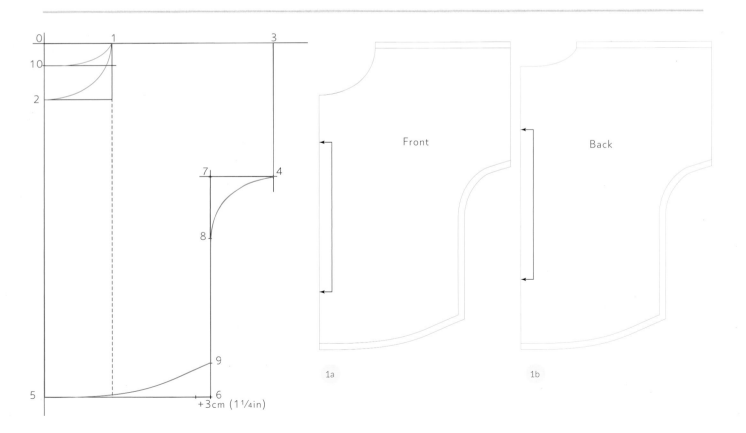

Front

Back

1a

1b

+3cm (1¼in)

FABRIC

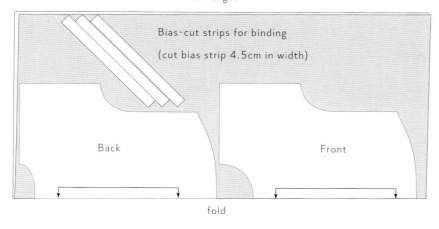

selvedges

Bias-cut strips for binding

(cut bias strip 4.5cm in width)

Back

Front

fold

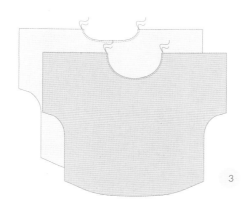

3

4

YOU WILL NEED

- 1.5m (1½yd) woven fabric, 150cm (60in) wide
- Matching thread
- Basic sewing kit (see Tools and Equipment)

PATTERN INVENTORY

- Front – cut 1 on the fold
- Back – cut 1 on the fold
- Bias cut strips for binding

1   Trace off the two pattern pieces, front and back, then add a 1.5cm (⅝in) seam allowance to the shoulder line, side seam and hem.

2   Cut out the pattern pieces, following the lay plan (see General Sewing Techniques: Cutting out).

3   Staystitch around the neckline on the front and back (see General Sewing Techniques: Machine stitching).

4   Place the front and back right sides together. Match up the shoulder seams and pin. Sew and neaten the seam allowances together (see General Sewing Techniques: Neatening seams). Press the seam to one side.

All seam allowances are 1.5cm (⅝in) unless otherwise stated.

5   Join all the bias strips together to make one long piece: Placethe first strip right side up horizontally. Place the second strip right side down vertically across the right-hand end of the first strip. Sew from top left to bottom right where the two strips cross (a). Trim the seam allowance to just under 1cm (⅜in). Press the seam open (b).

6   Measure around the neckline. Cut off a length of bias strip 2cm (¾in) longer than this measurement.

7   Join the short ends of the bias strip with a 1cm (⅜in) seam. Press the seam open. Fold the bias strip to find the mid and quarter points. Mark them with a pin or water-soluble marker.

8   Fold the neckline to find the centre back and centre front points, and mark with a pin or a water-soluble marker. Now fold to find the quarter points and mark in the same way.

9   With the right side of the binding to the wrong side of the top, match the binding seam to the centre back. Match up the rest of the centre and quarter points and pin in place.

10 Ease the binding around the neckline so that it sits neatly and pin it in place. Sew with an 8mm (a scant ⅜in) seam allowance. Press the binding up, away from the top.

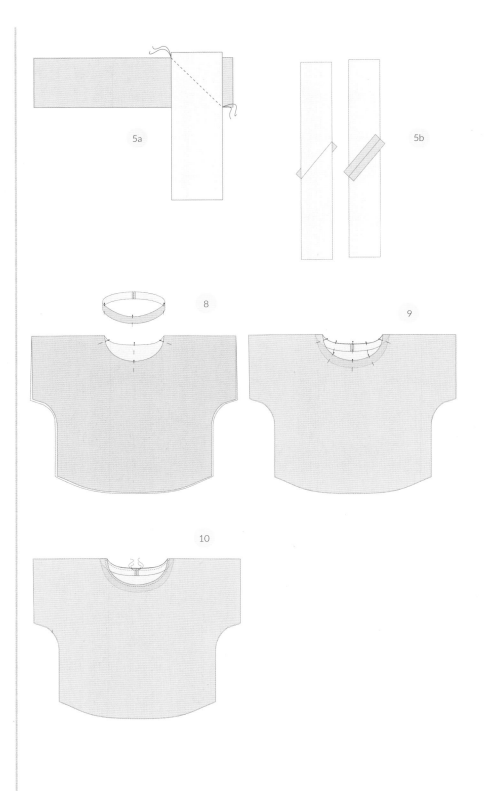

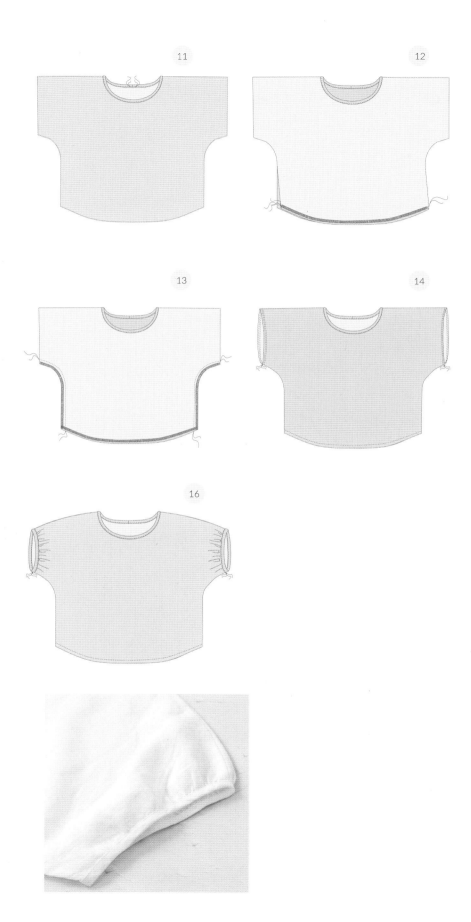

11 Fold the binding over the right side of the top and tuck under the raw edge so that it just covers the first row of stitching. Pin in place. Edge stitch the binding in place from the right side of the top (see General Sewing Techniques: Machine stitching). This means you can keep the finish nice and neat.

12 Neaten the curved hem edge and press 1cm (⅜in) to the wrong side. Topstitch in place (see General Sewing Techniques: Machine stitching) and press to finish.

13 With right sides together, sew the side seams and neaten the seam allowances together. Press the seam allowances to one side.

14 Starting and finishing at the side seam, sew a double row of long gathering stitches around the sleeve (see General Sewing Techniques: Machine stitching).

15 Measure loosely around your elbow while it's flexed. Cut two lengths of bias strip 2cm (¾in) longer than this measurement for the sleeve bindings.

16 Attach the sleeve bindings in the same way as the neck binding in step 6, lining up the binding seam with the side seam and the midpoint of the binding with the shoulder seam. Gently gather up each side of the sleeve to fit the binding. Spread the gathers out evenly, then stitch in place.

17 Finish the binding in the same way as the neckline. Any visible gathering threads can be gently removed by pulling them through with a pin.

Embroidered Tee

A little bit of simple embroidery can be a wonderful way to rest the mind. It allows you to slow down, take time out from your daily routine and forget about all those little niggles and worries for a while. The slow, repetitive nature of embroidery is almost like a kind of meditation in its own right, as it enables you to switch off from the hustle and bustle around you and focus on creating something beautiful.

This simple motif to decorate the neckline of the Woven Tee only uses three stitches: long and short stitch, stem stitch and French knots. For instructions on how to sew these stitches, see General Sewing Techniques: Basic embroidery stitches. I used five colours of thread to add a bit of variation to the flowers and leaves, but I kept the colours sympathetic to each other. However, you can go to town with whatever colours you like.

Fabric Choices

Embroidery can be done on almost any fabric,
provided you place the fabric in an embroidery hoop
to keep it taut as you sew.

- Woven tee
- Stranded embroidery thread (floss) in your chosen colours
- Tracing and copy paper
- Dressmaker's carbon paper
- Pencil
- Old ballpoint pen
- 20cm (8in) embroidery hoop
- Embroidery needle
- Embroidery scissors
- Thimble (optional)

EMBROIDERING THE TEE

1 To transfer the design onto your fabric, trace the design onto a piece of normal copy paper.

2 Make sure your tee is lying on a hard, flat surface, then place a sheet of dressmaker's carbon paper over the fabric where you want the design to go. Now position your tracing over the garment exactly where you want the design to be. I weight my design down, but you can pin it in place if you prefer. Using a ballpoint pen (I keep an old one that's run out of ink just for this), draw over the design with enough pressure to transfer the carbon onto your fabric.

3 When you have gone over the whole design (you may need to move the carbon paper slightly), place the fabric in an embroidery hoop. To do this, loosen the screw of the embroidery hoop slightly to separate the rings. Place the inside ring under the layer of fabric you're going to embroider and place the outside ring (with the screw) over the top. Slide the outer ring over the inner ring, trapping the fabric securely and making sure it is taut, then tighten up the screw. You won't be able to fit the whole motif in the hoop, so you'll be working on a small section at a time and moving the hoop along as required.

4 Pull off about 70cm (30in) of thread (floss) at a time so that it doesn't knot and separate it into two lots of three strands each. This makes it easier to work with, but if you prefer a bolder design you can work with all six strands; just remember to choose a needle that has a big enough eye to hold whatever thickness of thread you're using.

5 Work on a section of the design at time, taking the woven tee out of the hoop and moving it along as necessary; see General Sewing Techniques: Basic embroidery stitches. Start by embroidering the little circles on the edge of the garland in French knots, then go on to stitch the leaves, using long and short stitch for the leaves themselves and stem stitch for the stalks. Finally, embroider the flowers in long and short stitch.

6 When you have finished this first section, carefully move the hoop to another section to sew the rest of the design. Once the design is complete, remove the hoop and give the fabric a gentle steam from the reverse side, just to let it all sit back in place again.

Embroidery thread (floss) usually come as six strands in a skein. I like to wind my threads onto a wooden peg so that they are easier to wind off.

If your neck line is longer and you need more pattern, repeat another set of leaves at each end, or add another flower.

STITCH KEY

French knots

Stem stitch

Long and short stitch – leaves

Two-colour long and short stitch – flowers

Chocolate Orange Cake
& Homemade Mocha Latte

Chocolate Orange Cake

Who doesn't love chocolate and the fabulous endorphin rush it gives you? This is a complete indulgence and definitely one to treat yourself with. The tartness of the orange curd just cuts through the sweetness of the chocolate, making it a much more complex and grown-up cake.

INGREDIENTS

FOR THE CAKE

- 100g (3½oz) softened and unsalted butter, plus a little extra for greasing the tins
- 50g (1¾oz) good-quality cocoa powder
- 90ml (3 fl oz) boiling water
- 3 large free-range eggs
- 4 tbsp milk
- 175g (6oz) self-raising (self-rising) flour
- 1 rounded tsp baking powder sifted into the flour
- 300g (10½oz) golden caster (superfine) sugar
- Finely grated zest of 1 orange

FOR THE ORANGE CURD

- 2 large free-range eggs plus 2 extra yokes
- 225g (8oz) golden caster (superfine) sugar
- 2 large oranges, juiced and zested
- 2 tbsp lemon juice
- 115g (4oz) softened and unsalted butter cut into small cubes

FOR THE CHOCOLATE GANACHE

- 300ml (10 fl oz) double (heavy) cream
- 300g (10½ oz) good-quality dark chocolate – minimum 70% cocoa solids

METHOD

Preheat the oven to 180°C/350°F/gas mark 4. Grease two x 20cm (8in) round sandwich tins and line the bases with baking (parchment) paper.

TO MAKE THE SPONGES

Measure the cocoa and boiling water into a large bowl and mix to a paste. Add the remaining ingredients and beat again until combined. I use a food processor for this, but be careful not to overmix it.

Divide the mixture between the two greased and lined tins. Bake in the preheated oven for about 20–25 minutes until the sponges are well risen and shrinking away from the sides of the tin.

Remove the sponges from the oven and turn out of their tins onto a cooling rack. Leave to cool completely.

While the cakes are cooling, make the fillings.

TO MAKE THE ORANGE CURD

Beat the eggs and yolks together in a large bowl. Stir in the caster (superfine) sugar, orange zest and juice, lemon zest and cubes of butter.

Put the bowl over a pan of simmering water, making sure it doesn't actually touch the water. Stir with a wooden spoon until the butter has melted and the mixture is thick enough to coat the back of the spoon. Run your finger down the back of the spoon; if it leaves a path, the curd is ready. This is an excellent opportunity to have a quick taste!

Leave to cool completely, then pour into jars and cover. Store in the fridge, where it will keep for up to three weeks. This makes more than you will need for the cake, but then you have plenty left to lather over some hot toast later.

TO MAKE THE CHOCOLATE GANACHE

Gently heat the cream in a medium non-stick saucepan until hot but not quite simmering, stirring occasionally.

Pour the cream over the broken chocolate pieces. Stir once and leave to stand for 5 minutes. Stir the melted chocolate into the cream just enough to combine – don't over-stir or the mixture could become oily. Leave to cool for 10 minutes.

When the cakes are completely cool, spread a thick layer of orange curd onto the top of the bottom layer. Then spread about half of the chocolate ganache onto the underside of the top layer. Very carefully place the top layer on top of the bottom layer.

Cover the top of the cake with the other half of the chocolate ganache. Decorate with some squiggles of orange zest.

Homemade Mocha Latte

As we slide gently from winter to spring, the lighter mornings make me want to start my day outside. I find a hand-warming mug of homemade mocha latte is a wonderful way to start the day.

INGREDIENTS

- Approx. 45–50ml (2 fl oz) espresso or strong coffee
- 2 tsp cocoa powder (or hot chocolate powder, if you prefer it sweeter)
- Vanilla or peppermint essence, or maple syrup (optional)
- 1 cup of milk – cow, oat, almond or whatever kind you prefer
- Whipped cream
- Grated chocolate to finish

METHOD

Add the cocoa or chocolate powder to the coffee and mix well. Add vanilla or peppermint essence, or maple syrup, if you wish.

Heat and froth up the milk. Gently pour the milk over the coffee and chocolate mix and stir well.

Add gently whipped cream on top.

Dust with grated chocolate.

Summer

Palazzo Pants

These palazzo pants are a complete indulgence and totally fulfill my dream of wafting my way elegantly through the warm, lazy days of summer. Incredibly comfortable and easy to wear, they sit just that little bit higher on your waist to enable you to team them with a camisole or a shirred summer top. With wide trousers it's all about proportion, so they need to be paired with a more fitted or nipped-in shape on top.

These trousers have a proper fly, although this is a quick and nifty way of inserting it. I rather like these slightly more technical processes: I can switch off and completely immerse myself in what I'm doing, following each step and seeing the progress I'm making.

There is something decidedly decadent about really wide trousers. These are reminiscent of 1930s resort wear and I always think of Katherine Hepburn or Coco Chanel when wearing mine. Oh, to be as glamorous as they were..! I'll just have to sit on my steamer chair sipping a Long Island iced tea and imagine.

Fabric Choices

Palazzo pants need a fabric that will show off the grace and movement of the garment, so something like a soft linen or a viscose crepe would be ideal. Depending on how extrovert you want to be, a beautifully bright colour would be stunning – but there is enough fabric to really carry a bold print, too.

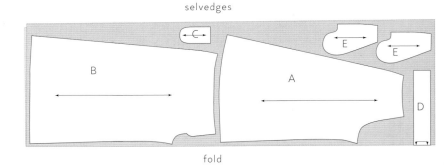

YOU WILL NEED

- 2.5m (2¾yd) light- to medium-weight woven fabric, 15cm (6in) wide
- 1m (1yd) lightweight iron-on interfacing
- 20-cm (8-in) zip
- Button, approx. 1.5–2cm (⅝–¾in) in diameter
- Matching thread
- Basic sewing kit (see Tools and Equipment)

PATTERN INVENTORY

- A Front – cut 2
- B Back – cut 2
- C Fly facing – cut 1
- D Waistband – cut 1 on the fold in fabric and 1 on the fold in interfacing
- E Pocket – cut 4

A LITTLE BIT OF PREP

1 Cut out the pattern pieces, following the lay plan (see General Sewing Techniques: Cutting out).

2 Transfer the pattern markings to your fabric (see General Sewing Techniques: Transferring pattern markings), paying special attention to the markings for the pleats.

3 Apply interfacing to the waistband (see General Sewing Techniques: Interfacing).

4 With right sides together, sew the trouser backs together along the back crotch. Neaten the seam allowances together and press to one side (see General Sewing Techniques: Neatening seams).

All seam allowances are 1.5cm (⅝in) unless otherwise stated.

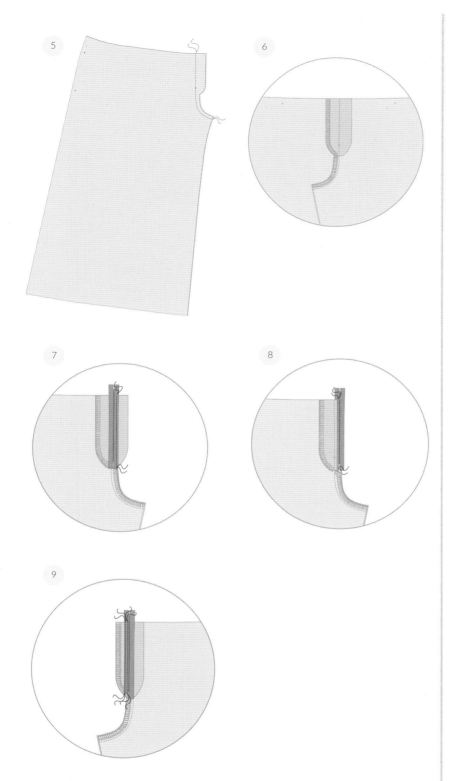

FLY ZIP

The fly extension is the curved section at the centre front of the two front pieces. The fly facing is a separate piece that prevents the zip from being visible when the pants are worn.

5   With right sides together, machine baste the fronts together from the waist to the large dot. Change the stitch length back to normal, sew a few reverse stitches and then sew the rest of the front crotch seam.

6   On the right-hand side of the fly extension, snip into the seam allowance just beneath the curve. Press open the machine-basted fly opening on the front and press the crotch seam to the left. Neaten the left-hand side of the fly extension and neaten both sides of the crotch seam allowance together.

7   Fold the right-hand side of the pants under to leave the unfinished side of the fly extension on its own. Lay the zip right side down along the right side of the centre front, so that the zip teeth are about 6mm (¼in) from the seam itself and the zip stopper is 1.5cm (⅝in) below the large dot. If the zip is too long and hangs over the top edge, that's fine as you can trim it back later on. Pin the zip to the fly extension only. Using a zip foot, sew along the right zip tape to hold the zip in place.

8   Fold the zip underneath the fly extension so that the fabric of the fly extension sits close to the zip teeth. Topstitch along the zip close to the zip teeth (see General Sewing Techniques: Machine stitching).

9   Open out the pants and let the right side of the fly extension, with the zip attached, flop over onto the left side. Fold the left side of the pants under so that the left side of the fly extension is on its own. Fold up the left end of the zip tape. Pin and sew along the zip tape close to the zip teeth. Sew a second row of stitching close to the edge of the zip tape.

10 Open the pants out flat, with the right side uppermost. Referring to the pattern, mark on the line for the fly topstitching. Following the marked line and using a normal foot, sew from the waist down and stop exactly on the large dot. Open up the basting stitches on the centre front and sew a small bar of satin stitch at the base of the zip on the large dot.

11 From the wrong side of the pants, trim back the excess fabric on the right side of the fly extension by about 1cm (⅜in).

12 Fold the fly facing in half, wrong sides together. Sew around the curved edge and neaten or overlock (serge) the two layers together.

13 From the wrong side of the pants, lay the fly facing over the whole fly section, aligning it with the curved lines of the fly extension. Line up the folded edge of the fly facing with the right side of the zip. Fold the right pants out of the way so that you can pin the fly facing in place. Using a zip foot, sew through the seam allowance only.

14 Secure the fly facing to the fly extension at the base and level with the large dot. Make sure you only sew through the fly pieces and do not catch in the pants.

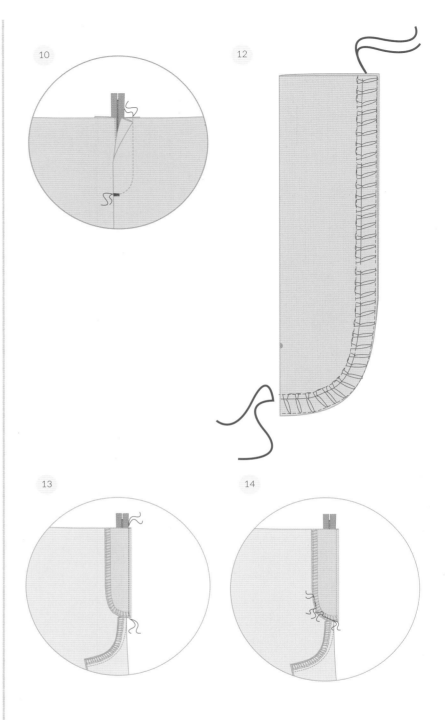

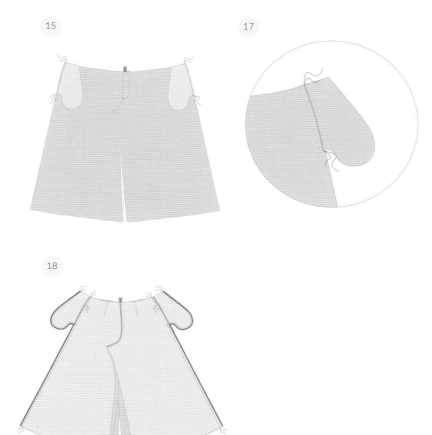

15 Matching the notches, with right sides together, place a pocket on each side of the fronts. Sew the pockets to the fronts with a 1cm (⅜in) seam allowance. Repeat on the backs.

16 Neaten the pocket seams on the backs, starting and finishing a little away from the pocket itself. There is no need to neaten the front pocket seams, as they will be hidden by the finished pocket.

17 Press the pockets away from the pants on both the front and back and understitch the pockets to the seam allowance (see General Sewing Techniques: Machine stitching).

18 Place the fronts and backs right sides together. Match up the waists, pockets and hems. Sew down the side seam to the first large dot. Then sew around the pocket, pivoting at the second large dot to sew down the side seam to the hem. Finish or neaten the seam. Repeat on the other side seam.

19 Match up the front and back crotch seams and pin together. Match up the hems and the notches. Pin and sew from just behind the crotch seam, over the crotch seam and down to the hem. Repeat for the other side of the inside leg seam, so that the stitching overlaps at the crotch, and then neaten the seam allowances together.

FINISHING THE WAIST

20 Fold the pleats following the pleat markings. Make sure you do this accurately, as it will affect how the waistband fits. Tack (baste) across the tops of pleats to hold them in place.

21 Neaten the long un-notched edge of the waistband. With right sides together, matching up the notches, side seams and centre front marks, pin the raw edge of the waistband to the waistline. The ends of the waistband should overhang the trousers by 1.5cm (⅝in). Pin and sew in place.

22 Press the waistband and seam allowance up away from the trousers. Trim off any excess overhang from the zip, then trim the waistband seam allowance down by half. Fold the centre front part of the waistband down on itself so the right sides are together and the neatened edge hangs past the waist seam by 1cm (⅜in). Stitch across the short edges of the waistband at the opening edges. Turn through to the right side and press flat.

23 Tack (baste) the rest of the waistband in place so that the neatened edge is 1cm (⅜in) below the waist seam. Sew around the waistband from the right side, stitching in the ditch of the waist seam.

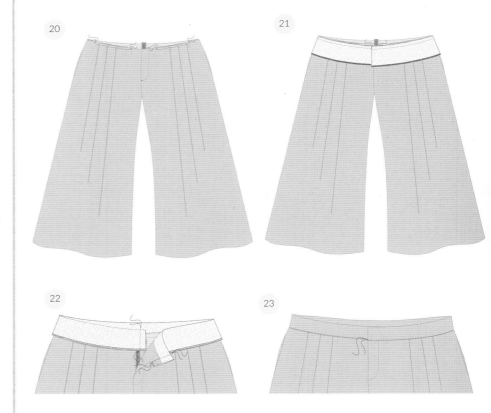

24 Centre the button on the waistband so that it sits in the middle of the fly shape. Mark where the buttonhole will sit; this will be the front end of the buttonhole. Sew the buttonhole back from this point. Attach the button so that it sits directly under the end of the buttonhole in the centre of the fly shape.

25 Check the finished length of your palazzo pants and trim off any excess; leave enough fabric for a 1.5cm (⅝in) hem. Neaten the raw edge, press up the hem and topstitch it in place.

Shirred Summer Top

Shirring is a wonderfully simple technique that involves sewing rows of stitching in parallel tramlines across the fabric, using elastic thread that makes it scrunch up beautifully. Like me, you will probably have fond memories of childhood summer dresses made in this exact same way. Some people call the technique 'mock smocking' — but it is so much quicker and easier than traditional smocking and much less labour intensive.

It's entirely up to you whether or not you add straps. Leave them off if you feel more like a '70s disco diva in a strapless number, or add delicate little shoestring ties if you feel more comfortable with a bit of something there. If you prefer a slightly more covered look, adding proper wide straps can make more of a statement.

The same technique can be used for tops and dresses — you just decide how much shirring you want to do. A band across the top and bottom can be just as effective as a whole shirred top.

Fabric Choices

This technique works much more effectively on lightweight fabrics such as cotton lawn or viscose rayon.

YOU WILL NEED

- Lightweight fabric (see Working out how much fabric you need)
- Matching thread
- Shirring elastic thread
- Basic sewing kit (see Tools and Equipment)

PATTERN INVENTORY

- Front – cut 1
- Back – cut 1
- Straps – cut 2

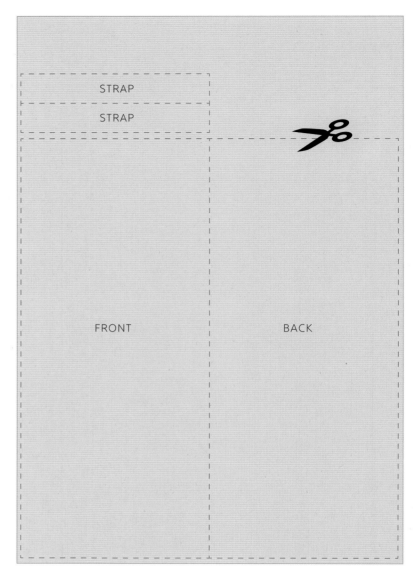

All seam allowances are 1.5cm (⅝in) unless otherwise stated.

PRACTICE MAKES PERFECT!

If you've never done shirring before, have a few practice attempts before you embark on this project. For shirring, you wind elastic thread onto the bobbin in place of the usual sewing thread. (Use regular thread in the needle.) The trick is to wind the elastic onto the bobbin without stretching it – but it cannot be loosely wound either. There is the 'Goldilocks' zone of elastic thread winding and this, I am afraid, only comes with practice. It pays to have a little play first and get used to the technique before you embark on your fist shirring project.

- Set up your sewing machine to sew a normal straight stitch, but increase the length to about 4–5.

- Insert the bobbin with the elastic thread and pull it up through the tension mechanism as normal.

- Thread up the machine with the colour of regular sewing thread that you want to be visible on the right side of the garment.

- Sew from the right side of the fabric, making sure you reverse your stitching at the start and finish of the row to secure the elastic thread. You can pull the top thread through to the underneath and tie the thread and elastic if you prefer.

- Space the rows about 1–2cm (½–¾in) apart. The more rows you sew, the more gathered the fabric will become.

- When you have finished the shirred section, gently hover a steam iron over the gathered section. This will help condense the shirring even more.

TROUBLESHOOTING!

- The elastic has pulled through!
  Make sure you reverse stitch or tie a knot in the thread ends and secure your sewing at the start and finish.

- It's not stretchy!
  Check how tightly the bobbin thread has been wound onto the bobbin. If it's too loose, it will not have used the stretch in the elastic, so rewind the bobbin with a bit more tension. If this doesn't work, try tightening the tension on the sewing machine slightly to make it harder for the elastic to pass through the mechanism.

- I can't keep a straight line!
  Draw on the lines to follow before you start sewing. I like to use a water-soluble pen, as it will just wash out.

WORKING OUT HOW MUCH FABRIC YOU NEED

1   Start by taking a few measurements:

- Bust
- Finished top length
- Finished strap length
- Finished strap width

2   Because shirring gathers up the fabric, the width of your fabric needs to be twice your bust measurement plus 3cm (1¼in) for the side seams. For example, my bust measurement is 107cm (42in), so my fabric needs to be 215cm (84in) wide plus 3cm (1¼in) − 218cm (85½in) in total. To work out the length of fabric you need, measure from just above the bust to wherever you want it to finish (usually between your waist and hips) and add 3cm (1¼in) for the hems. Cut two rectangles to this size − one for the front and one for the back.

3   Use whatever fabric is left over to cut the rectangles for the straps. Decide how long and wide you want the straps to be. Add 4cm (1½in) to the length; double the width and add 2cm (¾in). Cut two rectangles to this size; you can use the selvedge of the fabric as a guide to get the angles just right.

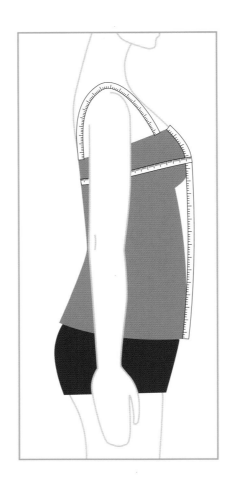

You can cut the straps whatever width you like. Generally thinner straps are fine if you don't have bra straps showing, but I prefer slightly wider ones to cover them up. But, hey: you're making this top, so go with whatever works for you. I cut my straps 8cm (3in) wide so that they would be 3cm (1¼in) wide when finished.

Tip

Most fabrics are either 114 or 140–150cm (44 or 55–60in) wide – so unless you're making the top for a child, you will probably need to sew two lengths of fabric together to create a piece that's wide enough.

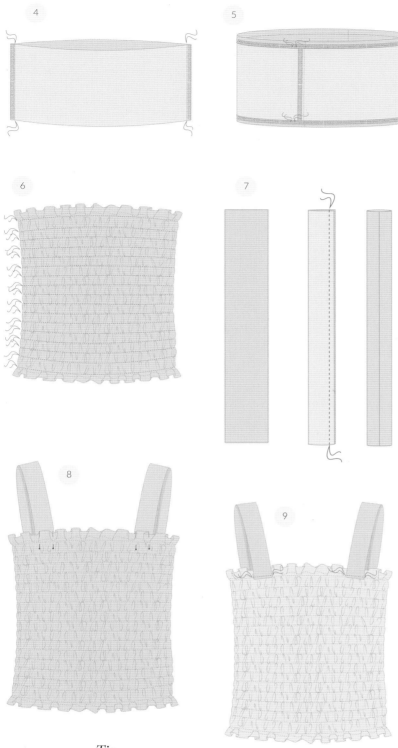

4 Place the rectangles for the front and back right sides together and sew down the short sides to form a tube. Neaten the seam allowances (see General Sewing Techniques: Neatening seams) and press to one side.

5 Neaten the top and bottom edges of the fabric tube and press 1.5cm (⅝in) to the wrong side. Topstitch the hems at the top and bottom (see General Sewing Techniques: Machine stitching). Turn the tube right side out. Press flat.

6 Now you can start shirring. Set up your machine with elastic thread in the bobbin and normal sewing thread in the top. Start just below the top hem and finish just above the bottom hem so that you are only sewing through one layer of fabric. Sew as many rows as you need to around the tube of fabric, spacing them about 2cm (¾in) apart.

7 Fold the straps in half widthways, right sides together, and sew along the long unfolded edge, taking a 1cm (⅜in) seam allowance. Turn the straps right side out and press so that the seam is in the middle.

8 Pin the straps in place on the wrong side of the top and try the top on. Adjust the straps if necessary so that they are in the correct position.

9 Tuck under 1cm (⅜in) at the end of each strap and sew in place.

Tip

You will need to change your bobbin regularly, so wind a few with elastic thread in advance.

Cami and Shorts

Sometimes something is just too good to throw away, even when it's out of style or slightly damaged. I love the idea of giving old things a new purpose by turning them into something else. It means I can enjoy them just that little bit longer and I'm doing my bit to 'Make Do and Mend'.

This lovely camisole and shorts set makes use of an old duvet cover, although an old sheet or tablecloth would work just as well. Slightly worn duvet covers have a wonderful softness to them, making them ideal to transform into underwear or something comfy to sleep in.

There are no darts: all the pieces are cut on the bias, so the shaping comes from the 'give' in the fabric and it will mould itself to your shape.

Fabric Choices

Because the pattern pieces for the cami and shorts are cut on the bias, soft, fluid fabrics work better as they will drape and flow over the body. A super-soft cotton lawn would be ideal, or a luxurious silk crepe de chine or a silk charmeuse if you're feeling like treating yourself.

YOU WILL NEED

- Old sheet, duvet cover or tablecloth
- About 1m (1yd) of soft picot-edged elastic, 1cm (⅜in) wide
- Matching thread
- Basic sewing kit (see Tools and Equipment)

PATTERN INVENTORY

- A Cami front – cut 1
- B Cami back – cut 1
- C Cami front facing – cut 1
- D Cami back facing – cut 1
- E Cami strap – cut 1
- F Shorts front and back – cut 2

(flip the shorts pattern to cut a right and left leg for the pair)

A LITTLE BIT OF PREP

1   Cut out the pattern pieces›, following the lay plan (see General Sewing Techniques: Cutting out). Be sure to follow the grainlines: the pieces will look as if they're placed at odd angles, but don't worry. Make sure you flip the shorts pattern – or better still, trace off two patterns so that you have a right and a left.

2   Transfer the pattern markings to your fabric (see General Sewing Techniques: Transferring pattern markings).

3   Stay stitch around the neckline and underarms of the back and front camisoles and facings (see General Sewing Techniques: Machine stitching). Fabric that's cut on the bias has a lot of stretch, or 'give', in it; the stay stitching will ensure that the fabric does not stretch out of shape.

All seam allowances are 1.5cm (⅝in) unless otherwise stated.

FABRIC

selvedge

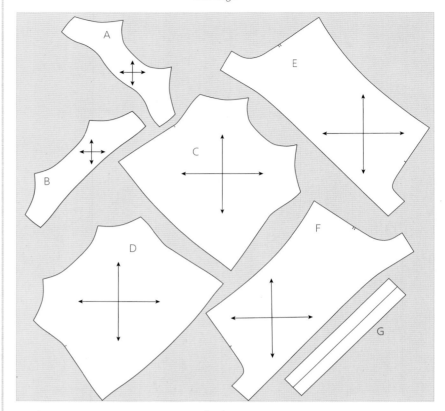

selvedge

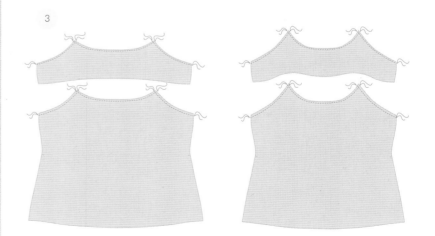

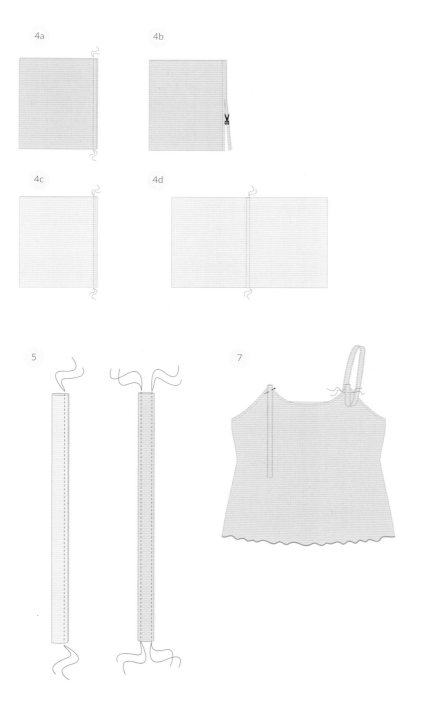

4a

4b

4c

4d

5

7

CAMISOLE

The side seams are sewn using a French seam, which means that the raw edges are completely enclosed and do not need to be neatened.

4 Place the front and back wrong sides together and sew the first side seam, using an 8mm (a scant ⅜in) seam allowance (a). Trim the seam allowances by just under half and press the seam flat (b). Fold the garment so that the right sides are together and the first seam lies along the crease. Press in place. Sew another seam to enclose the raw edges (c). This seam should be wide enough to just cover the seam allowance but not so wide that you can see any stray threads from the first seam. Press the seam flat, then press it to one side (d). Repeat with the second side seam.

5 Fold the strap in half with right sides together and sew along the long unfolded edge, taking a 5mm (¼in) seam allowance. Repeat with the second strap. Turn the straps right side out and press flat. You can use a loop turner or just sew some long threads inside the strap and gently pull on them from the other end to turn the strap through. You can also edge stitch each long edge if you wish (see General Sewing Techniques: Machine stitching).

6 Hem the camisole using a decorative stitch on the overlocker (serger) or a narrow double-fold hem.

7 Place the end of the strap on the right side of the camisole front so that the strap hangs down and one end is level with the point. Pin in place. Now flip the strap over to the back and do the same. Try on the camisole to see if the straps are the correct length and adjust if necessary. Machine baste across the straps to attach the ends to the camisole.

8   Place the facing pieces right sides together and sew down the side seams. Press the seams open. Neaten the bottom edge by overlocking or turning up an 8mm (a scant ⅜in) hem and topstitching it in place.

9   With right sides together, matching up the front and back points of the camisole with those on the facing, place the facing over the camisole. Tuck the straps down, so that they lie underneath the underarm, and match up the side seam of the facing with the side seam of the camisole. Starting at a side seam, sew around the neckline of the camisole, pivoting and sewing across each strap and then pivoting again to continue around the neckline. Make sure the straps don't get caught in the stitching. Trim and clip around the seam to release the tension in the curves and reduce the bulk at the corners

10 Understitch as far as you can around each section of the neckline (see General Sewing Techniques: Machine stitching). Then turn the facing to the inside of the camisole and press everything nice and flat. If you have some spare buttons or a bit of ribbon, you can add a bit of decoration, too.

SHORTS

The crotch seams are sewn using a French seam, like the camisole side seams. The inside leg seams of the shorts are sewn using a flat felled seam. Both these methods enclose the raw seam edges.

1   Stay stitch around the waist edge of the shorts (see General Sewing Techniques: Machine stitching).

2   Lay the two shorts pieces on top of each other. Sew up the front and back crotch seams using a French seam (see Camisole: Step 4).

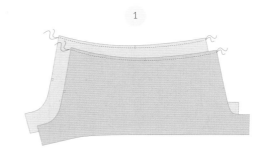

3 Open out the shorts. With right sides together, match up the inside leg seams and sew a 1.5cm (⅝in) seam (a). Press the seam open and trim back one side of the seam allowance by 1cm (⅜in) (b). On the untrimmed seam allowance, press under 6mm (¼in). Fold the pressed-under seam allowance over the trimmed one (c). Sew close to the edge of the folded-over seam allowance to enclose the trimmed seam allowance. Press flat (d). This is known as a flat felled seam.

4 Measure the elastic around your wait so that it fits comfortably, allowing for a 2cm (¾in) overlap. Cut the elastic to size, then overlap the ends and sew a square to hold the two ends together. Make sure you don't twist it!

5 Mark the quarter, half and three-quarter points on the elastic. These will match up with the centre front, centre back and side notches of the shorts. Place the right side of the elastic ring over the right side of the fabric at the waist of the shorts, so that the raw edge of the waist is level with the plain edge of the elastic. Match up all the marks and seams and pin or clip in place. You can add in extra pins as you gently stretch the elastic to fit the shorts.

6 Sew a stretch stitch or small zigzag stitch along the bottom edge of the elastic close to the decorative edge. If any fabric is visible, you can carefully trim off under the elastic.

7 Fold over the elastic so it is just hidden from the right side. Now sew a triple-step zigzag, a long, wide zigzag, from the right side to hold the elastic in place. The stitch should cover most of the width of the elastic.

8 Hem the shorts using a decorative stitch on the overlocker or a narrow pin hem that you can sew on an ordinary sewing machine.

Lemon Drizzle Cake
& Elderflower Cordial

Lemon Drizzle Cake

Passed down from my grandma to my mum, this is the easiest cake in the world: you basically bung everything in together and mix it up. I love the 'weigh your eggs' method my grandma used, as it makes everything so simple and you don't even have to remember any quantities.

MAKES ONE 20CM (8IN) SQUARE CAKE

INGREDIENTS

FOR THE CAKE

- 3 large free-range eggs
- Softened and unsalted butter or margarine
- Self-raising (self-rising) flour
- Caster (superfine) sugar
- Zest of 2 unwaxed lemons
- Juice of 1 unwaxed lemon

FOR THE DRIZZLE

- Juice of 1 unwaxed lemon
- 4 tbsp caster (superfine) sugar

METHOD

Preheat the oven to 180°C/350°F/gas mark 4. Grease a 20cm (8in) square cake tin. Instead of lining the tin with baking (parchment) paper, I cheat and use a massive cake case and just plop that inside the cake tin. It also helps to hold in all the lovely juicy drizzle.

Weigh the eggs still in their shells, then crack them into a large mixing bowl. Weigh out the same amount each of sugar, fat and flour, and add that to the eggs along with the lemon zest and juice.

Using an electric mixer, blend all the ingredients together until light and creamy looking.

Bake for 50–60 minutes or until a wooden skewer inserted in the middle of the cake comes out cleanly, checking in the last 5 minutes to make sure that it doesn't overbake.

Elderflower Cordial

While the cake is still hot and in the tin, mix the lemon juice and caster (superfine) sugar for the drizzle together until most of the sugar has dissolved. Poke lots of holes all over the surface of the cake with a skewer and then gently spoon over the drizzle.

Leave to cool in the tin and it will create the most lemony, moist sponge cake with a zingy, crisp topping – although, to be honest, I can rarely wait that long; I like to serve mine warm with a little creme fraiche.

There is nothing so wonderfully refreshing on a hot, dry summer's day as a glass of cool elderflower cordial. Select flowers that have just opened or are about to, to make sure they have plenty of pollen. Use them as soon as you can after picking for the best results, although you can freeze them to use later. I use a bit of citric acid in my recipe as it makes the cordial last that little bit longer and gives it a much more refreshing flavour, too.

MAKE ABOUT 1.5–2 LITRES (3–4 PINTS) OF CORDIAL

INGREDIENTS

- 20–25 flowerheads with the stalks trimmed
- 1.5l (3 pints) water
- 85g (3 oz) citric acid (you should be able to find this in your local chemist)
- 2 unwaxed lemons, sliced
- 2.5kg (5½ lb) sugar

METHOD

Put the flowerheads, water, citric acid and sliced lemons into a large saucepan and bring to boiling point. Let it bubble for a couple of minutes and then cover and allow to cool and infuse overnight.

Strain the liquid through a scalded muslin (cheesecloth) and return to the pot.

Add the sugar and slowly bring to the boil, allowing the sugar to dissolve. Simmer for 5 minutes.

While still hot, decant into sterilized bottles or jars. You will need to protect your hands, as the glass will get very hot.

Once the bottles are filled, seal with a sterilized flip-top, screw lid or even a cork. As the cordial cools, it will create a seal with the lid to keep it lovely and fresh.

Store in a cool dark place or in the fridge once opened. You can dilute to taste with still or sparkling water and just drop in a slice of lemon and an ice cube or two.

To sterilize my glass bottles, I usually put them through the dishwasher or hand wash them in hot soapy water, then rinse and dry them completely in a low oven.

Autumn

Oversized Shirt

Everyone needs an oversized shirt for this time of year. Many years ago I used to pinch my Dad's to wear layered up over various band T-shirts, but now I can make my own. This design works in all seasons, as you can choose fabrics that keep you cool in summer and warm in winter.

I love the process of shirt making! It can be quite technical, but the slow consideration that goes into sewing this kind of project is incredibly rewarding. This particular shirt has a convertible collar, meaning that it can be worn either buttoned up or open, so it's a lovely one to start with if you are new to making shirts.

This project may take you several sewing sessions, so I like to batch similar processes or steps together to make things more streamlined. I have done this with the instructions to help you work in a similar way.

Fabric Choices

This shirt would work in a soft denim or checked plaid, but I prefer linen. If you wish, you can use a contrasting fabric for the inner yoke.

- 2.3–2.5m (2½–2¾yd) main fabric, 150cm (60in) wide
- 25cm (10in) contrasting fabric for the inner yoke (optional)
- 50cm (20in) lightweight iron-on interfacing
- Matching thread
- 8 buttons 1.5–2cm (⅝–¾in) in diameter
- Basic sewing kit (see Tools and Equipment)

- A Front – cut 2
- B Back – cut 1 on the fold
- C Yoke – cut 2 on the fold (you can use a contrast fabric for the inner yoke if you prefer)
- D Collar – cut 2 on the fold in fabric and 1 on the fold in interfacing
- E Front facing – cut 2 in fabric and 2 in interfacing
- F Sleeve – cut 2
- G Sleeve tabs– cut 4
- H Pocket – cut 2

All seam allowances are 1.5cm (⅝in) unless otherwise stated.

FABRIC

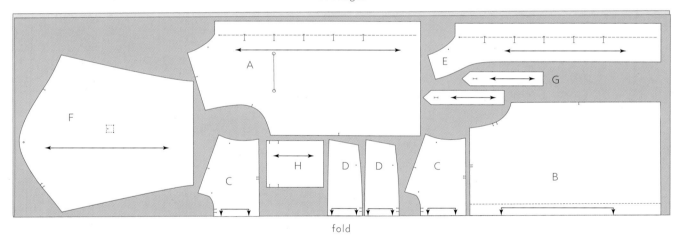

INTERFACING

3a

3b

4

6

8

A LITTLE BIT OF PREP

1   Cut out the pattern pieces, following the lay plans (see General Sewing Techniques: Cutting out).

2   Transfer the pattern markings to your fabric (see General Sewing Techniques: Transferring pattern markings).

3   Apply interfacing to the upper collar and front facing pieces (a) (see General Sewing Techniques: Interfacing). Stay stitch around the neckline on the front facings, shirt fronts and yoke pieces (b) (see General Sewing Techniques: Machine stitching). Finish the outer edges of the facings.

POCKETS, COLLAR AND PLACKETS

4   Neaten the top edges of the pockets. Fold over the tops of the pockets along the fold line so that the right sides are together. Taking a 1cm (⅜in) seam allowance, sew across the short ends to create a facing.

5   Turn the pocket facing right side out and winkle out the corners. Press under the seam allowances around the sides of the pockets, mitring the corners. Work two rows of topstitching across the bottom of the pocket facing to hold it in place (see General Sewing Techniques: Machine stitching).

6   Place the pockets on the shirt fronts along the placement lines. Topstitch in place with two rows of stitching, reinforcing the top corners with box stitching.

7   Trim 3mm (⅛in) from the outer edge and short sides of the under collar. This makes it roll under slightly for a better finish to the collar.

8   With right sides together, centre the under collar on the inner edge of the upper collar. Ease the under collar out to fit the upper collar. Pin and sew along the outer edge of the collar. Trim the seam allowance down to 5mm (¼in) and trim off the corners (see General Sewing Techniques: Reducing bulk).

9 Turn the collar right side out and carefully press it flat so that the seam is just on the edge. Topstitch the collar from the right side for a bit of extra detail and decoration, working two rows of stitching.

10 Place a pair of sleeve tabs right sides together. Sew around with a 1cm (⅜in) seam allowance, leaving the straight short edge open (a). Clip off the corners (b). Turn right side out, winkle out the corners and press flat. You can topstitch around the point for added detail if you wish. Mark and sew buttonholes to fit your buttons (see General Sewing Techniques: Buttonholes and buttons) (c). Repeat with the second pair of tabs.

BACK YOKES AND FRONT FACINGS

11 Match up the pleat markings on the on the shirt back, fold the fabric along the lines in the direction of the arrows and press to create a box pleat. Machine baste across the pleat, inside the seam allowance, to hold it in place.

12 With right sides together, matching up the notches along the yoke line, lay the outer yoke over the shirt back. Pin and sew together. Press the yoke and the seam allowance up, away from the shirt back.

13 With right sides together, matching up the notches along the shoulders, lay the shirt fronts over the outer yoke. Pin and sew together along the shoulder seams. Press the yoke and seam allowances away from the shirt front.

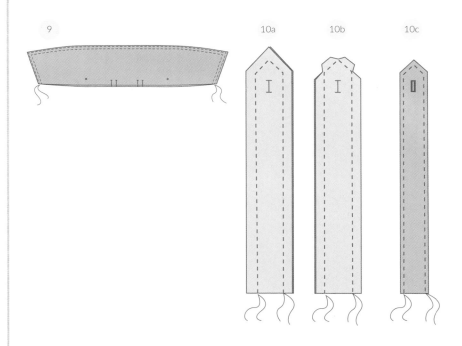

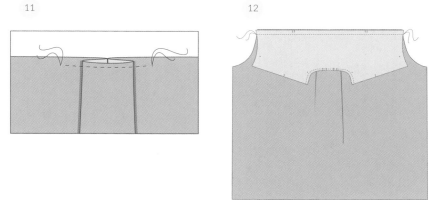

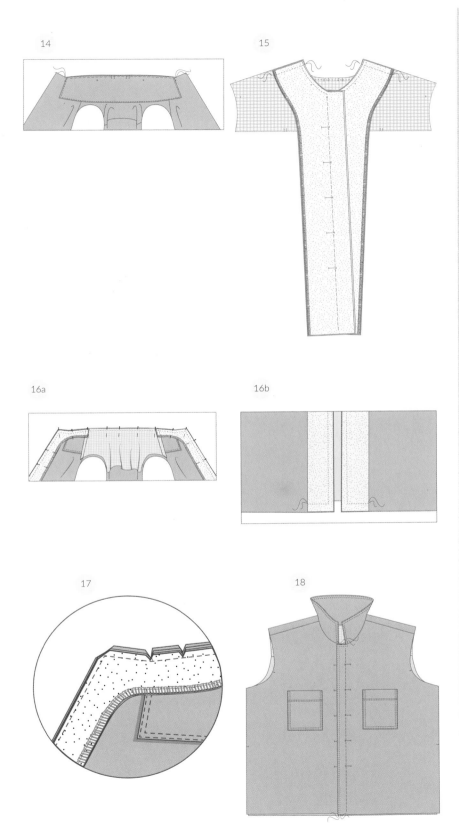

14 With the under collar next to the right side of the yoke, place the collar on the back neckline. Pin together, matching up the notches and making sure the front edge of the collar sits on the small dots on the shirt fronts. Machine baste in place.

15 With right sides together, lining up the neck edge and the edge of the facing with the notches at the shoulders, pin the front facings to the inner yoke. Sew the seams and press towards the yoke.

16 With right sides together, place the inner yoke and front facing on the shirt. You will create a sandwich, with the collar as the filling (a). Pin and sew all the way around – across the bottom of the facing at the hem, up one side of the front, around the neckline, back down the other front edge and across the facing at the hem (b). Be sure to pivot at the corners and at the small dots at the ends of the collar.

17 Clip the corners and layer the seam allowance of the facing. Snip into the curved neck seam allowance to release the tension in the seam and allow the neck to sit flat. Trim back the hem of the front facing to 1cm (⅜in).

18 Turn out the collar and front facings to the right side. Carefully winkle out the corners and roll the seam so that it sits right on the edge. Give it a good steam and press. Work two rows of topstitching from the hem up the front edge and around the corner to meet the topstitching on the collar. Do the same on both edges of the front opening.

19 With the shirt back right side up in front
    of you (a), roll up the back until it sits on
    top of the yoke (b). The yoke seam will be
    visible. Fold the inner yoke out over the
    collar and rolled-up shirt back to meet the
    back yoke seam. Pin together, lining up
    the notches, and sew across the back yoke
    seam through all three layers (c).

20 Carefully pull the roll of fabric out through
    one of the gaps between the inner and
    outer yoke pieces at the armhole. Keep
    gently pulling it through until the whole
    shirt has turned itself right side out. It will
    seem like a never-ending task, but just
    keep going: it will work!

21 Once turned through, flatten out the yoke
    and press along the bottom seam where
    it joins the shirt back. Topstitch from the
    right side along the seam line on the yoke.
    At the shoulder seams, press under the
    seam allowance on the inner yoke so that it
    just covers the shoulder seam. Pin in place
    and topstitch from the right side.

SLEEVES AND TABS

22 Press under 1cm (⅜in) on the short, open
    edge of the first tab. Place this folded
    edge to the top placement marks on the
    wrong side of the sleeve. Sew in a square
    between the placement dots (a). On the
    right side, sew the button just above the
    centre of the stitched square (b). Repeat
    with the second tab.

23 Place the sleeve, with the large dot sitting
    on the dot on the yoke that marks the
    shoulder line. Walk the sleeve around
    the armhole so that the underarm seams
    match and the notches line up, then pin
    in place. Sew and neaten the seam. Press
    towards the body of the shirt. Repeat with
    the second sleeve.

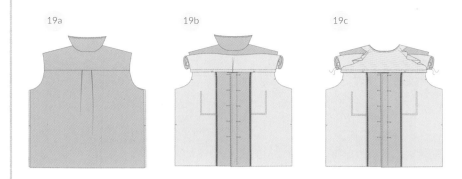

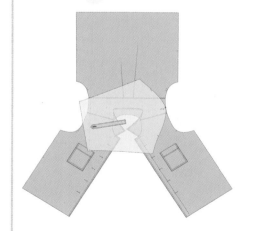

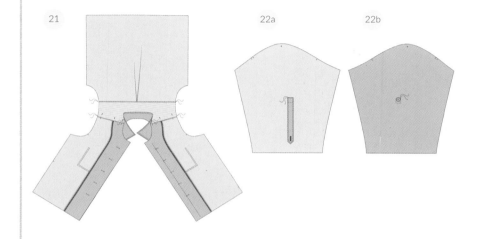

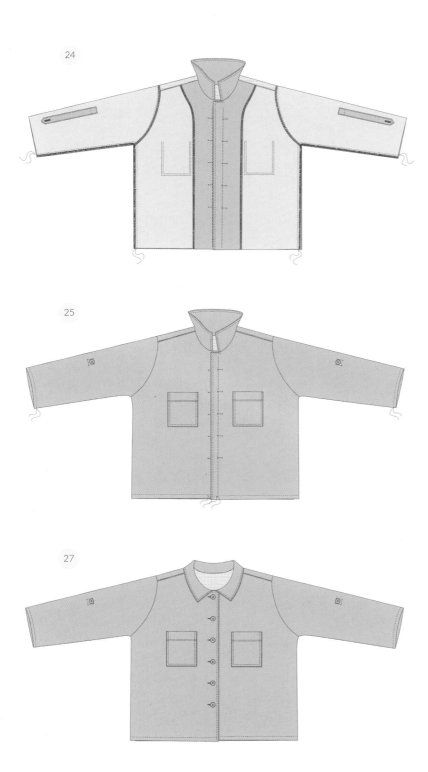

24 Fold the shirt inside out and sew up the underarm seams, matching up the cuffs, armhole seams and side notches. Neaten the seams and press towards the front.

HEMS AND BUTTONS

25 Press up the hems on the sleeves and shirt by 1cm (⅜in), then press up again by 1.5cm (⅝in). Topstitch around the sleeves and hem.

26 Using the pattern markings as a guide, transfer the buttonhole lines onto the right-hand side of the shirt front. Make sure they are in the correct place for you; adjust them if necessary.

27 Sew buttonholes the correct size for your buttons and carefully cut them open (see General Sewing Techniques: Buttonholes and buttons). Lay out the shirt and mark the button positions through the buttonholes along the centre front line. Sew on the buttons in the correct places.

Classic T-shirt

It really doesn't matter what time of year it is, a classic T-shirt will serve you well. Whether you want to wear it over a vest in the summer or under a shirt in the cooler months, T-shirts are a wardrobe staple.

Once you've nailed the basic construction, they are very simple to put together. I like to batch make several at a time, almost like a factory production line. It makes me feel organized and efficient to work on a particular process for several garments at a time.

Fabric Choices

This T-shirt is made from jersey fabric. Many people shy away from sewing with jersey or knit fabrics, but really there is nothing to be scared of. An overlocker (serger) will make things easier, as the 'give' in the overlocker stitch allows the fabric to stretch without snapping the stitching threads. However, you can sew jersey fabric on a normal sewing machine if you use the correct needle – a stretch or ballpoint needle will push between the yarns rather than piercing them and a walking foot will help prevent the fabric from stretching as you sew.

YOU WILL NEED

- 1.5m (1⅝yd) light- to medium-weight single jersey, 140cm (55in) wide
- Stay tape or iron-on bias tape
- Matching thread
- Basic sewing kit (see Tools and Equipment)
- Twin needle (optional)
- Overlocker (serger) – or ballpoint needle if using a sewing machine

PATTERN INVENTORY

- A Front – cut 1 on the fold
- B Back – cut 1 on the fold
- C Sleeve – cut 2
- D Neckband – cut 1

FABRIC

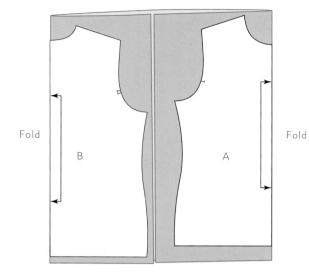

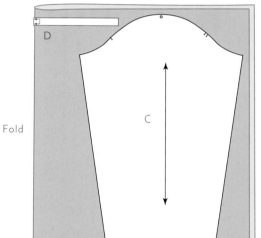

All seam allowances are 1.5cm (⅝in) unless otherwise stated.

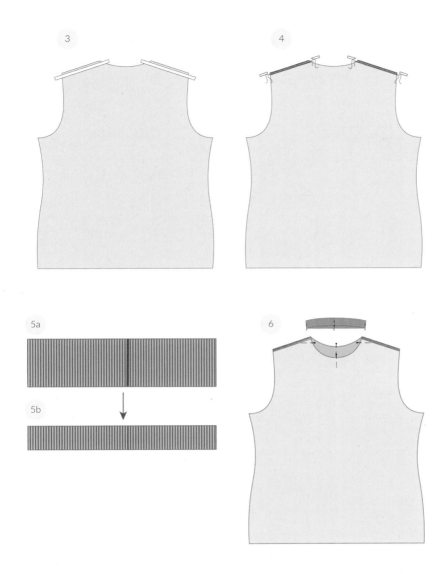

If you are using iron-on bias tape, make sure that the rough or glue side is placed on the fabric with the offset chain stitch furthest away from the cut edge of the T-shirt fabric. Gently press it in place to adhere it to the T-shirt fabric. If you are using stay tape, make sure that the tape runs along the seam line and pin in place.

A LITTLE BIT OF PREP

1   Cut out the pattern pieces, following the lay plans (see General Sewing Techniques: Cutting out).

2   Transfer the pattern markings to your fabric (see General Sewing Techniques: Transferring pattern markings).

3   Lay out the back of the T-shirt with the wrong side uppermost. Apply a length of stay tape or bias tape along each shoulder, leaving them hanging about 2cm (¾in) over each end of the shoulder seam. This will ensure that the shoulders don't stretch out of shape while wearing.

SHOULDERS

4   Place the back and front right sides together. Match up the shoulders and pin or clip together. Sew or overlock (serge) across the shoulders, making sure you capture the stay or bias tape along the line of sewing. Trim off the excess tape flush with the edge of the shoulder. Press the seam towards the front.

NECKLINE

5   Fold the neckband in half widthways, right sides together, and sew across the short ends to form a tube (a). Press the seam to one side, then fold the neckband in half lengthways to enclose the seam. Press all the way around to create a doubled-over neckband (b).

6   Mark the quarter, half and three-quarter points on both the neckband and the neckline of the T-shirt with pins. Turn the T-shirt inside out and then lower the neckband into the neckline so that the raw edges line up. Match up the marking pins, then pin the neckband to the neckline, gently stretching it to fit the neckline as you go.

7   You can hand tack (baste) the neckband in place now if you prefer – or just go for it and sew or overlock around the neckline (a). Remove any tacking stitches and press the seam down towards the body of the garment (b).

8   Using a cover-stitch machine or a topstitch with a sewing machine and twin needle, sew around the neckline to hold the seam in place (see General Sewing Techniques: Using a twin needle). Turn the top through to the right side Give the whole neckline a gentle steam and press to help it retain its lovely curved shape.

SLEEVES

9   With right sides together, match up the dot on the sleeve head with the shoulder seam and pin in place (a). Walk the sleeve around the armhole so that the single notches match up, pinning in place as you go. Do the same around the back of the sleeve, matching up the double notches. Sew or overlock around the sleeve head (b). Press the seam towards the sleeve.

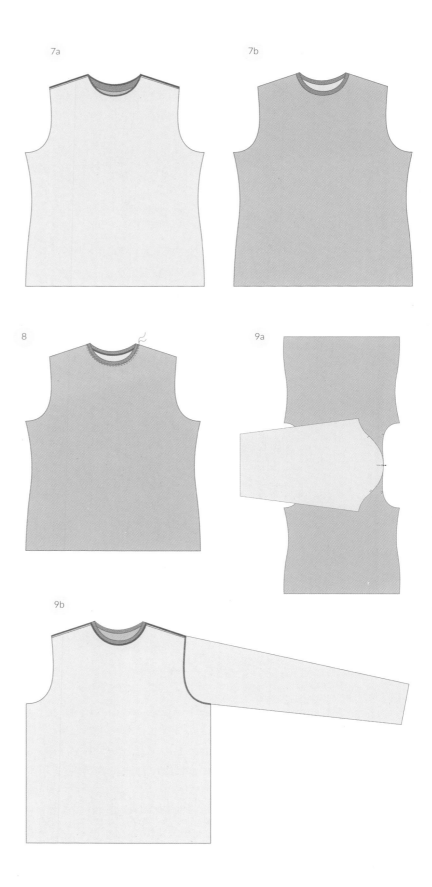

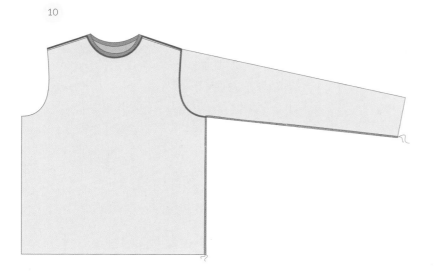

10

11

10 With right sides together, match up the side seams, lining up the cuffs, armhole seam and waist hem. Pin or clip in place. Working from the waist upwards, sew or overlock (serge) the side and underarm seams in one continuous seam, matching up the key points on the way.

HEMS

11 Press under the hems on the sleeves and the waist. Topstitch with a twin needle, coverstitch machine or decorative stitch to hold the hems in place. Give everything a gentle steam and press to allow the fabric to relax back into the correct position.

Reloved Blanket

Although sorting out clothing that you no longer wear can be cathartic, it's rather a wrench to throw away something you really love. I find this especially so for woolly, comfy things. With this project, you can wrap yourself up in a blanket made of things you used to wear and enjoy.

Reusing loved and treasured items is a wonderful way to prolong their life. Without sounding too 'woo woo', I do feel a sense of gratitude for the comfort a garment has given me while I'm chopping it up. I know it has served its current purpose and is going to become something else that I will love and cherish.

Fabric Choices

This method makes use of all types of knitted loveliness, not just 100% wool items that can be washed and felted. If you have a lightweight knit, you can always double up the layers to make that part of the blanket a similar weight to the others.

- A selection of loved and worn knitted jumpers or cardigans
- Matching thread
- Contrasting yarn for blanket stitching
- Basic sewing kit (see Tools and Equipment)
- Yarn needle

1 If you can, gently unpick the knitted items so that you can lay the front, back and sleeves out flat. If that's tricky, carefully cut through the seams.

2 Measure the knitted areas that are usable on each garment and decide how big you want to cut the squares for your blanket. I like to keep them as large as I can to make the most of any patterns or designs on the knitted garments.

3 Mark out the squares with a 1cm (⅜in) seam allowance around each one.

4 With a matching thread, machine baste 5mm (¼in) just inside the marked seam allowances. This will prevent the knitted fabrics from unravelling when you cut out the squares.

5 Cut out all the squares from all the knitted garments and arrange them in your desired pattern.

All seam allowances are 1cm (⅜in) unless otherwise stated.

6

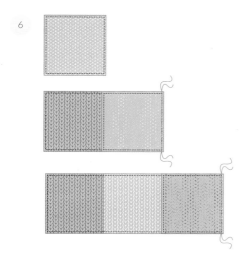

7

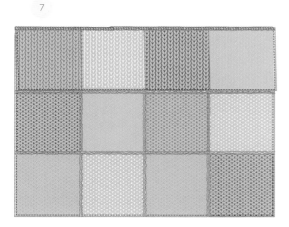

8

6   Start by joining all the squares from one row. With right sides together, sew a seam along the line of machine basting, making sure you reverse stitch at the start and end of each seam. Once you've joined all the rows, sew each row to its neighbour in the same way.

7   Even though the blanket has been sewn together, you still have raw edges on the back. To neaten this, pinch up the seam from the right side on the first row and blanket stitch through all the layers (see General Sewing Techniques: Basic embroidery stitches), using a yarn needle and a contrasting colour of yarn. This will enclose the raw edges of the seam underneath and give a lovely decorative finish on the right side of the blanket, too. Blanket stitch all the horizontal rows first, then the vertical ones. When you get to a cross seam, push the first one flat and blanket stitch over it to hold it in place. I like to do the blanket stitch in a contrasting colour, but you can use whatever you have to hand.

8   To finish the outside edges, fold a small hem to the wrong side all the way around and blanket stitch over it.

Spiced Sugar Crust Apple Cake
& Hot Cider Nog

Spiced Sugar Crust Apple Cake

We make this cake as a way of using up the glut of apples we have in the garden. It's wonderful served cold, but it works just as well as a warm pudding with vanilla ice cream. It freezes well, too, so you can make a couple and keep one to brighten up a cold rainy afternoon. I love the idea of saving up things to make you smile when your future self needs something lovely.

MAKES ONE 18CM (7IN) ROUND CAKE

INGREDIENTS

- 200g (7oz) self-raising (self-rising) flour
- 1½ tsp ground mixed spice
- 200g (7oz) softened and unsalted butter
- 200g (7oz) soft brown sugar
- 4 large free-range eggs, beaten
- 4 small eating apples, such as Cox's Orange Pippins, peeled, cored and diced to whatever size you like
- 1 large eating apple, cored and cut into wedges
- Demerara sugar, for creating the crusty topping
- ½ tsp cinnamon

METHOD

Preheat the oven to 180°C/fan 350°F/gas mark 4. Liberally grease an 18cm (7in) round cake tin. Line with baking (parchment) paper or place a really big paper cake case inside if you prefer.

Stir the ground mixed spice into the flour. Place all the remaining ingredients except the apple, demerara sugar and cinnamon in a large bowl or food mixer. Beat together by hand or in a mixer for a couple of minutes until everything is completely combined.

Stir the diced apple into the mix. You can decide how chunky you want your bits of apple to be.

Hot Cider Nog

Spoon the cake mixture into the prepared tin and arrange the wedges of apple over the top in concentric circles. Add the cinnamon to the demerara sugar and mix together. Sprinkle over the top.

Bake in the oven for 55–60 minutes or until a skewer inserted in the middle of the cake comes out clean.

Allow the cake to cool in the tin for a few minutes before turning out onto a wire rack. Cool completely before slicing and serving.

In this recipe, I've blended two of my favourite seasonal beverages in one satisfying glass: the heat of spiced cider and the comforting creaminess of homemade eggnog. It's like drinking warm, spiced custard – total heaven! If you don't want it to be too alcoholic, you can leave out the whisky or rum.

SERVES 4–6, DEPENDING HOW CHILLY YOU ARE

INGREDIENTS

- 500ml (18fl oz) single (light) cream
- 250ml (9fl oz) milk
- 310ml (10fl oz) apple cider
- 2 large eggs
- 250g (9oz) sugar
- 2 tbsp brown sugar (this makes all the difference in flavour!)
- ¼ tsp salt
- ¼ tsp ground cinnamon
- ¼ tsp freshly grated nutmeg, plus more for topping
- Shot of whisky or rum per adult
- Whipped cream for topping

METHOD

Whisk together the single (light) cream, milk, cider, eggs, sugars, salt and spices in a large bowl until blended. Place the bowl over a pan of barely simmering water and continue to whisk until the mixture thickens slightly and will coat the back of a wooden spoon. Go slowly with this, as you don't want to end up with scrambled eggs! Remove from the heat and carry on whisking for another minute or two.

Stir in the alcohol (or add it to individual glasses).

Ladle out into latte glasses if you have them or just plain old mugs. Add a dollop of whipped cream on top and a dusting of fresh nutmeg. Cup your hands around the mug, sip with your eyes closed and let out a satisfied 'hmmmmmm'!

Winter

Winter Coat

When it's time to reach for a winter coat, it's like welcoming back an old friend. A good-quality coat can last a decade if it's treated well and looked after, so this is a wonderful project to take your time with and make the most of, because you will get many years of wear out of it.

This is one of those projects where you really don't want to stint in terms of fabric quality. It is definitely worth saving up and using a superb-quality fabric if you can. I have been known to completely unpick a large gent's coat just because I loved the fabric and wanted to re-make it, but that's for another project.

I do love a coat with a bit of extra space inside it, either for adding yet another woolly layer or for hiding a small child in when playing hide and seek while walking in the woods. A capacious overgarment just adds to that delicious feeling of being wrapped up in a large, woollen hug.

Fabric Choices

The ideal fabric is a boiled wool, but any medium- to heavyweight woven fabric would work. Choose a fabric that has a bit of flexibility to it and is not too stiff, as this is a casual type of garment. If you cannot wear wool, a viscose mix would be great; as long as it is a woven and not a knitted fabric you will be fine.

YOU WILL NEED

- 2.8m (2⅛yd) main fabric, 150cm (60in) wide
- 2m (2¼yd) lining fabric
- Scrap of flannel or cotton wadding (batting) about 30cm (12in) long for the sleeve heads
- 1.2m (1⅜yd) medium-weight interfacing
- Matching thread
- 5 buttons, 2cm (¾in) in diameter
- Basic sewing kit (see Tools and Equipment)

PATTERN INVENTORY

- A Front – cut 2
- B Back – cut 2
- C Sleeve – cut 2 main fabric and 2 in lining fabric
- D Upper collar – cut 1 on the fold in fabric and 1 on the fold in interfacing
- E Under collar – cut 2
- F Pocket – cut 2 in main fabric
- G Front facing – cut 2 in fabric and 2 in interfacing
- H Back facing – cut 1 on the fold in fabric and 1 on the fold in interfacing
- I Front lining– cut 2 in lining fabric
- J Back lining– cut 1 on the fold in lining fabric
- K Pocket lining – cut 2 in lining fabric

MAIN FABRIC

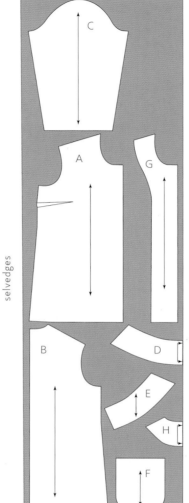

LINING FABRIC

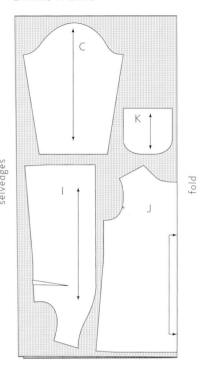

INTERFACING

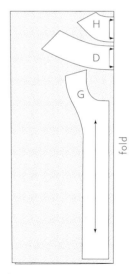

All seam allowances are 1.5cm (⅝in) unless otherwise stated.

1   Cut out the pattern pieces, following the lay plans (see General Sewing Techniques: Cutting out).

2   Transfer the pattern markings to your fabric (see General Sewing Techniques: Transferring pattern markings).

3   Apply interfacing to the upper collar, back facing and front facing pieces (see General Sewing Techniques: Interfacing). Stay stitch around the necklines of the front (a) and back (b) pieces, the front and back facings (c), and the back lining (d) (see General Sewing Techniques: Machine stitching). Also stay stitch around the notched corner at the front hem.

4   Sew the darts in the front coat pieces. Press the darts upwards.

5   Place the two back pieces right sides together and sew down the centre back seam. Press the seam open.

6   Trace off a crescent shape from the sleeve head pattern in flannel or cotton wadding. It should be about 3cm deep at the apex and should start and finish either side of the notches. This is stitched in after the sleeve and will slightly pad out the sleeve head to avoid any puckers or dimples.

BLUFF POCKETS

These are magic pockets, as you don't see any of the stitching from the right side. You can, of course, just topstitch the pockets in place if you prefer.

7   With right sides together, match up the pocket lining with the top edge of the pocket. Sew across the top of the pocket and press the seam down towards the lining.

8   Pull the lining down to line up with the bottom edge of the pocket and press across the top to create the pocket facing. Neaten the curved edge of the pocket and then sew a row of long easing stitches around the curve (see General Sewing Techniques: Machine stitching).

9   Press under the 2cm (¾in) seam allowance around the curved edge of the pocket, using the easing stitches to help pull up the excess fabric. Gently steam flat from the right side.

10 Place the pockets on the placement lines on the coat fronts and machine baste very close to the edge all the way around the curved edge.

11 Pull the pocket away from the coat to expose the seam allowance inside. Sew from the top, inside the pocket on top of the seam allowance, following the exposed stitches of the machine basting all the way around the curved inside edge of the pocket (a). This is slightly tricky to do, as you will only be able to sew a small section at a time. Secure your stitching at the start and finish. Fold down the corner of the seam allowance inside the pocket and secure with a small row of sewing (b).

SHOULDER AND SIDE SEAMS

12 With right sides together, lining up the shoulders and side seams, place the fronts on the back. Pin and sew together, then press the seams open.

7

8

11a
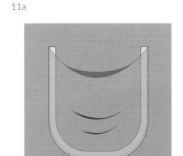

11b
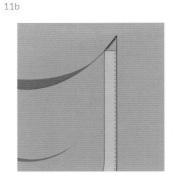

12
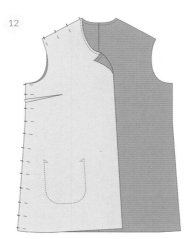

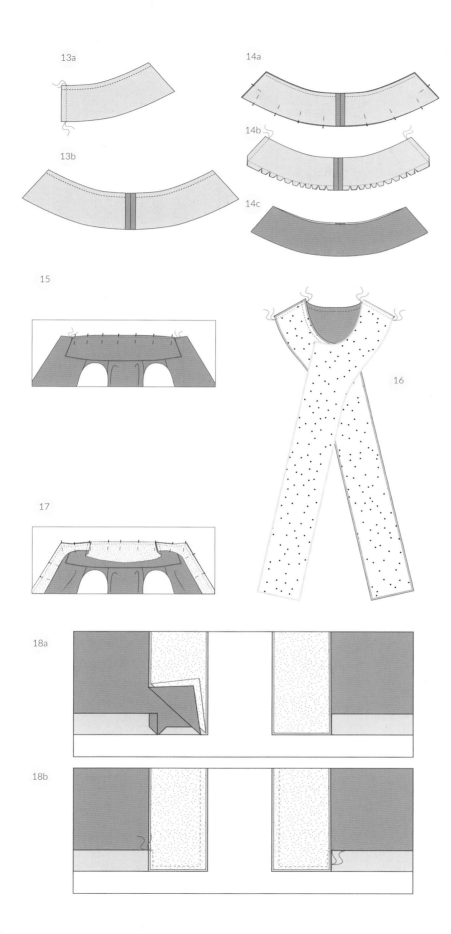

COLLAR AND FACING

13 With right sides together, sew across the centre back seam of the under collar (a). Press the seam open (b).

14 With right sides together, place the under collar on top of the upper collar (a); it will be slightly smaller, so ease it out to fit around the long edge of the upper collar. Pin and sew around the outer edge of the collar. Trim, clip and layer the seam allowances (b). Turn the collar through to the right side and press, making sure none of the under collar is visible from the top side (c).

15 With the under collar against the right side of the coat, place the collar on the neck of the coat. Pin, matching up the notches and making sure that the front edge of the collar sits on the small dot at the front edge. Machine baste in place.

16 With right sides together, sew the front facings to the back facing at the shoulders. Press the seams open.

17 With right sides together, place the facing on the coat; you will create a 'sandwich', with the collar as the filling. Match up the shoulder seams and notches, then pin the facing in place.

18 At the front hem, clip into the stay-stitched cut-out corner so that it will turn the corner of the facing (a). Sew from the bottom edge of the front facing, pivot at the corner to turn and sew across the bottom edge, pivot again to sew up the front edge around the neckline and back down the other side, pivoting at the corners and the small dots at the ends of the collar (b).

19 Clip the corners and layer the seam allowances (see General Sewing Techniques: Reducing bulk). Snip into the curved neck seam allowance to release the tension in the seam and allow the neck to sit flat. Trim back the hem of the front facing by half.

20 Turn right side out. Starting and finishing about 10cm (4in) from the centre front line, understitch through the facing and the neck seam allowance; this will help the collar to lie properly. Also understitch along the centre front through the facing and seam allowances, starting as close as you can to the hem and sewing up to 20cm (10in) below the front neck point.

SLEEVES

21 Sew a row of long easing stitches across the sleeve head 5mm (¼in) away from the cut edge of the fabric. Fold the sleeves in half, right sides together. Pin and sew the underarm seam. Press the seam open. Repeat with the second sleeve.

22 With the sleeve right side out and the coat inside out, slot the sleeve into the armhole. Match up the underarm seam with the side seam and the small dot on the sleeve head with the shoulder seam. Line up the single notches at the front and the double notches at the back. Pin in place and ease the rest of the sleeve in to fit the armhole. Sew all around the armhole. Repeat with the second sleeve.

23 Lay the flannel or wadding (batting) sleeve head over the sleeve, matching up the shoulder dots. Pin in place and then flip over to sew so that you can follow the original line of sewing. This will provide some support for the sleeve head and prevent it from dimpling when the coat is worn.

21

22
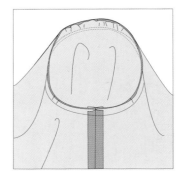

23
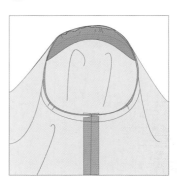

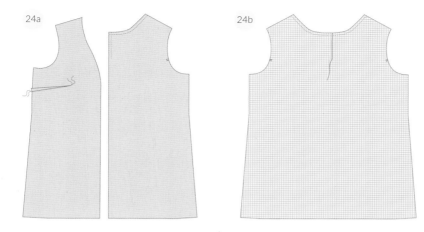

24a　24b

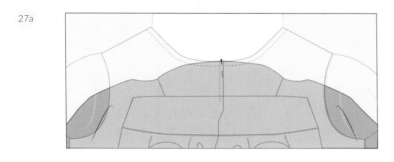

27a

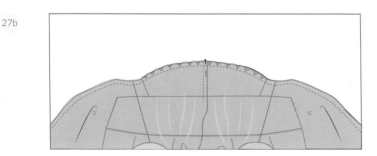

27b

24 Sew the darts in the front lining pieces and press them upwards (a). Fold the back lining in half, right sides together, then sew down the pleat line to the small dot. Press the pleat to one side (b).

25 With right sides together, matching up the shoulders and side seams, place the front lining pieces on the back lining. Sew and press the seams open, as in step 12.

26 Make up and insert the sleeves into the lining pieces, as in steps 21–22.

27 Place the lining to the back neck facing with the right sides together. Match up the shoulder seams, the notches and the small dots at the hem, and pin in place (a). Sew from the corner of the front facing up the front and around the facing back to the other side (b). Clip and press the seam towards the lining.

28 Press up the hems on the sleeves and coat and herringbone stitch them in place (see General Sewing Techniques: Hand sewing). Press under the 1.5cm (⅝in) seam allowance on the coat lining and sleeve lining hems and pin in place over the coat and sleeve hems. Slipstitch in place around the hems of the sleeve and coat. There will be a little extra pleat at the base of the front facing, so arrange it to sit nice and flat.

29 Using the pattern markings as a guide, transfer the buttonhole lines on to the right-hand side of the coat. Make sure they are in the correct place for you; adjust them if necessary. Sew buttonholes the correct size for your buttons and carefully cut open the buttonholes (see General Sewing Techniques: Buttonholes and buttons). Lay out the coat and mark the button positions along the centre front line, through the buttonholes. Sew on the buttons by hand.

Drawstring Trousers

These trousers are like secret pyjamas! You are wearing normal daytime clothes but they feel so comfy, just as if you're in your PJs.

These drawstring trousers are a very easy and capacious pair of pants – with numerous pockets, of course. I prefer to go for the elasticated option with the additional drawstring to add a bit of detail, but the choice is yours.

That's the wonderful thing about making your own clothes: making something to your own specifications and fabric choice is incredibly rewarding. When you're asked where you got 'such and such' and you reply, 'This? Oh, I made it myself', you can pop that warm and fuzzy feeling in the Happiness Jar and save it for later.

Fabric Choices

This style an be made in a whole range of fabrics. Here I've used a linen and cotton mix check, but a soft needlecord would also be lovely for the cooler months.

YOU WILL NEED

- 1.5–2m (1⅝–2¼yd) medium-weight woven fabric, 150cm (60in) wide
- 10–20cm (4–8in) contrasting fabric for inside the waistband (optional)
- Scrap of interfacing (optional)
- Matching thread
- 2–2.5m (2¼–2¾yd) twill tape, 1cm (⅜in) wide
- Basic sewing kit (see Tools and Equipment)

PATTERN INVENTORY

- A Front – cut 2
- B Back – cut 2
- C Waistband – cut 2 on the fold
- D Pocket – cut 4

A LITTLE BIT OF PREP

1   Cut out the pattern pieces, following the lay plans (see General Sewing Techniques: Cutting out).

2   Transfer the pattern markings to your fabric (see General Sewing Techniques: Transferring pattern markings).

3   If you are going to use a drawstring, apply a small square of interfacing to the waistband just under the markings for the buttonholes (see General Sewing Techniques: Interfacing). This will support the fabric when you cut it to create the buttonholes.

All seam allowances are 1.5cm (⅝in) unless otherwise stated.

FABRIC

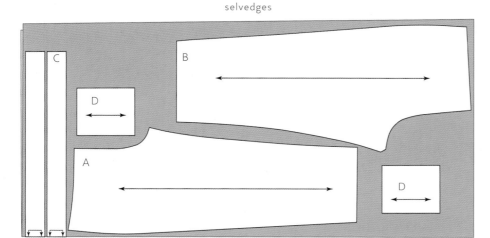

selvedges

fold

4

5

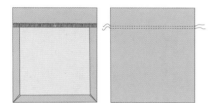

6

7

8

LEGS

4   Place the trouser fronts right sides together, then pin and sew along the front crotch seam. Neaten the seam allowances together and press to one side (see General Sewing Techniques: Neatening seams). Repeat with the back pieces.

POCKETS

5   Neaten the top edges of the pockets. Fold over the tops of the pockets along the fold line so that the right sides are together. Taking a 1cm (⅜in) seam allowance, sew across the short ends to create a facing. Turn the pocket facing right side out and winkle out the corners.

6   Press under the sides of the pocket and across the bottom. Mitre the corners. Topstitch across the top of the pocket to keep the facing in place (see General Sewing Techniques: Machine stitching).

7   Position the pockets on the trouser fronts and backs along the placement lines. Starting at the bottom of the pocket facing, topstitch in place, pivoting at the corners, until you get to the top edge. Pivot at the corner and sew three stitches across the top, then pivot again and sew a parallel line all the way around the pocket inside the first row. Pivot again at the top and sew across three stitches. Pivot and sew down the pocket to join up to where you started.

SEAMS

8   Place the trouser front and back right sides together. Pin and sew down the side seams. Pin and sew down the inside leg seams. Neaten the seam allowances together and press towards the front.

WAISTBAND

9   Sew a pair of buttonholes on the outer waistband in the marked positions and carefully cut them open (a) (see General Sewing Techniques: Buttonholes and buttons). Fold the outer waistband in half lengthways, right sides together, and sew across the short sides to form a circle. Press the seam open (b). Repeat for the inner waistband, omitting the buttonholes.

10 Place the two waistbands right sides together, matching the seams, then pin and sew around the top edge (a). Trim the seam allowance down by half and press it open (b).

11 Fold the waistband so that it's the right way around, with the inner fabric on the inside of the circle. Edge stitch around the top of the waistband though all layers (see General Sewing Techniques: Machine stitching). This will help to prevent the elastic from twisting as you wear the trousers.

Omit the next two steps if you just want a drawstring.

12 Measure the elastic around your waist so it fits comfortably, allowing for a 2cm (¾in) overlap. Cut the elastic to size, then overlap the ends and sew a square to hold the two ends together. Make sure you don't twist it.

13 Tuck the elastic inside the waistband and pin the raw edges together to hold the elastic in place. You will need to shuffle the fabric of the waistband around to do this. Gently stretch the elastic to allow the fabric of the waistband to sit flat.

9a

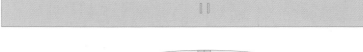

9b

10a

10b

14

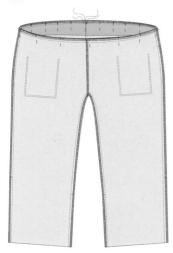

16

14 Turn the trousers inside out and lower the waistband into the trousers so that the raw edges line up, matching up the centre front and back seams with the notches and balance marks. Pin and sew in place. Neaten the seam allowances together.

15 Press up a 1cm (⅜in) hem, followed by a 1.5cm (⅝in) hem on the trouser legs. Topstitch in place.

16 Push a safety pin through the end of the twill tape and thread it through the buttonholes and all the way through the drawstring channel in the waistband. You can either hem the ends of the tape or just tie a knot.

Christmas Stocking

Everyone needs a Christmas stocking, regardless of their age. It's a tradition in our house that the stockings get put out on Christmas Eve. When the children were little, it was a real ceremony making sure that Father Christmas knew exactly where their stocking was to be found at the end of their beds. As they have got older, the stockings are now hung on their bedroom door handles waiting to be filled with an assortment of edible treats to be consumed before breakfast. Decadence is a feature of Christmas celebrations, after all.

I do enjoy a sense of ritual at certain times of the year. They are reassuring and remind us of people and places that are dear to us and we want to remember, allowing us to feel gratitude for what we have and who we can count on within our inner circle to give us succour and support.

Making and giving away what we make is an act of love, and this project is a wonderful way to show your love for someone. You can personalize the stocking by adding an appliqué letter or shape for that special person.

Fabric Choices

There is an abundance of Christmassy fabrics to choose from, mainly in craft cotton which makes up very easily. But you could go to town and make a more sumptuous stocking in velvet or brocade and decorate it with furnishing trims or tassels. You could also line the stocking with coordinating printed fabrics.

YOU WILL NEED

- 50cm (20in) main fabric, 114cm (45in) wide (a basic craft cotton)
- 25cm (10in) contrast fabric (for the toe and stocking top)
- 50cm (20in) lining fabric (I used calico)
- Contrasting fabrics or felt for the appliqué shapes
- Scrap of fusible bonding web
- Approx. 15cm (6in) ribbon for the hanging loop
- Approx. 15cm (6in) of fancy tape or ribbon for decoration
- Basic sewing kit (see Tools and Equipment)

PATTERN INVENTORY

- A Stocking – cut 2
- B Stocking top – cut 2
- C Stocking toe – cut 2
- D Stocking lining – cut 2

A LITTLE BIT OF PREP

1   Using the template in the templates section, cut out the pattern pieces (see General Sewing Techniques: Cutting out).

2   Transfer the pattern markings to your fabric (see General Sewing Techniques: Transferring pattern markings).

PREPARING THE STOCKING PIECES

3   Lay the contrast toe section over each main fabric stocking piece and sew in place with a zig-zag stitch over the top edge. Machine baste around the toe itself to hold both layers together.

4   Match up the stocking and stocking top, then flip the stocking top down so that the right sides are together and the raw edges are level. Sew across the seam, then fold the stocking top back up again. Press the seam open.

All seam allowances are 1.5cm (⅝in) unless otherwise stated.

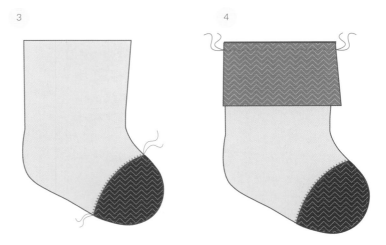

Tip

If you are using a letter or shape that has a particular direction, trace it off in reverse so that the letter or shape will be the right way round when you apply it to the stocking.

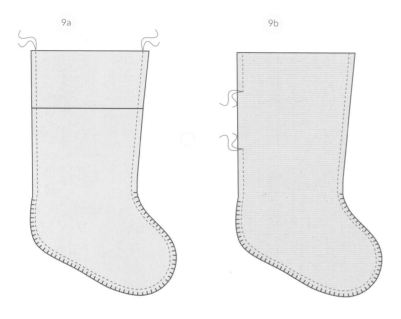

9a   9b

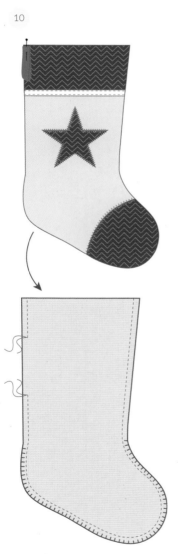

10

ADDING THE DECORATION

5   Sew a fancy ribbon or tape across the stocking top seam and add any other trimmings you like.

6   Trace the appliqué star shape from the Templates section onto the smooth, paper side of a piece of fusible bonding web and roughly cut it out. Place the rough, glue side of the bonding web on the back of the appliqué fabric, cover with a pressing cloth to diffuse some of the heat, and fix in place with a hot iron.

7   Carefully cut around the appliqué design and use a pin to scrape the back of the paper to release it. Peel off the paper backing, leaving the glue attached to the appliqué shape.

8   Place the appliqué shape in the correct position on your main stocking, cover with a pressing cloth and fix in place with a hot iron. Once your shape is firmly attached, you can outline it by hand or machine with some decorative stitching.

ASSEMBLING THE STOCKING

9   Place the front and back stockings with the right sides together. Starting at the top edge, sew all round the stocking shape leaving the top open. Clip and notch the seams, turn the stocking right side out and press (a). Repeat with the front and back linings, leaving an 8cm (3in) gap along the back edge so that you can turn the stocking right side out at the end (b).

10 Place the stocking inside the lining, right sides together. Fold the ribbon for the hanging loop in half and tuck it down in between the stocking and the lining at the back seam. Pin and stitch around the top edge of the stocking, catching in the hanging loop.

11 Pull the whole stocking through the gap in the lining seam, slipstitch the gap in the lining closed (see General Sewing Techniques: Hand sewing) and tuck the lining back down into the stocking. Give everything a good press.

Rich Fruit Cake with Hidden
Surprises & Mulled Wine

Rich Fruit Cake with Hidden Surprises

As the days shorten, I find myself wanting to hunker down and take my time with the pleasurable things in life, including baking. This is another family recipe, passed down from my great grandmother. The 'hidden surprises' are marzipan balls hidden beneath its surface: we take turns to push the balls into the cake mixture and make a wish with each one.

MAKES ONE 20CM (8IN) CAKE

INGREDIENTS

- 400g (14oz) currants
- 250g (9oz) sultanas
- 250g (9oz) raisins
- 150ml (5fl oz) rum or brandy
- 225g (8oz) softened and unsalted butter
- 225g (8oz) dark muscovado sugar
- 4 eggs, beaten
- 1 tbsp black treacle
- 350g (12oz) plain (all-purpose) flour
- 2 tsp mixed spice
- 75g (2¾oz) almonds (I like to leave the skins on, but you could use blanched ones if you prefer)
- 75g (2¾oz) glacé cherries
- 100g (3¼oz) mixed candied peel
- Zest of one lemon and one orange
- 200g (7oz) marzipan, either homemade or shop bought

METHOD

Prepare your cake tin first as this requires a little attention. The cake needs long slow baking so to prevent the outside becoming too dry it needs a bit of extra protection.

Line a 20cm (8in) cake tin with a double layer of baking parchment. Then create a baking collar by laying out a length of tin foil long enough to wrap around the tin. On top of this, lay a folded over length of moistened kitchen roll, then bring the foil over to encase the damp paper. Wrap this around the cake tin and secure with string. Preheat the oven to 160°C/325°F/gas mark 3.

Place the currants, sultanas and raisins in a bowl. Heat the rum or brandy until it just starts to bubble around the edge of the pan, then pour it over the fruit. Cover and allow to soak overnight.

Beat the softened butter and sugar together until pale and fluffy, making sure to beat out any lumps in the sugar. Gradually add in one egg at a time, beating well after each addition. Next beat in the treacle.

Sift the flour and mixed spice into the bowl and fold in gently. Then add the soaked fruit, almonds, cherries, peel and lemon and orange zest and mix until everything is combined.

Carefully spoon into the prepared tin, making sure not to allow any drips as these will burn.

Chop up the marzipan and roll it into grape-sized balls. Then gently push them into the cake mixture in concentric circles, making sure they are fully submerged.

Level off the top, but leave a slight dip in the middle. Loosely cover the top of the cake with a double layer of baking parchment with a hole cut in the middle. This will help prevent the top of the cake from becoming too dark.

Bake for 1 hour, then reduce the oven temperature to 140°C/275°F/gas mark 1 and cook for a further 1–2 hours or until a skewer inserted into the centre comes out clean.

Leave to cool in the tin for 30 minutes, then turn out onto a wire rack to cool completely.

Mulled Wine

What could be better for the soul than raising a glass with your nearest and dearest, whether it's at a New Year's Eve party or just a social get-together? You can keep this recipe on the straight and narrow or allow it to veer off the righteous path, depending on your company or how quickly you want to slide off the sofa.

THIS IS A PARTY-SIZED QUANTITY, SO REDUCE THE AMOUNTS TO SUIT THE OCCASION.

INGREDIENTS

- 2 clementines
- 1 lemon
- 1 lime
- 200g (7oz) caster (superfine) sugar
- 5 whole cloves
- 1 cinnamon stick
- A whole grated nutmeg
- 2 fresh bay leaves
- 1 vanilla pod
- 2 star anise
- 2 bottles of good red wine
- ½ bottle rum (optional)
- ½ bottle of whisky (optional)

METHOD

Cut the clementines, lemon and lime in half. Juice one half of each fruit and slice the other half. Add the juice and slices to a large pan or stockpot. Mix in the sugar and spices and just enough wine to cover it all.

Gently bring to the boil and stir until all the sugar has dissolved. Then add in the rest of the wine, and the whisky and rum, if using.

Bring to the boil again and then gently simmer for 15–20 minutes. Serve hot in glasses with handles.

General Sewing Techniques

Cutting out

Using pins to attach the paper pattern to the fabric is one way of laying out your pattern pieces. But you can also use weights to hold the pattern flat and then draw around the pattern with tailor's chalk or marker pens. This can be a bit quicker than using pins, but you must remember to cut inside the marked line or you risk adding in extra fabric to the pattern piece and potentially altering the size and accuracy of your pattern.

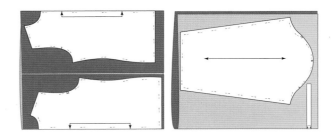

Transferring pattern markings

Transferring pattern information such as darts and button or pocket positions to the fabric is key to ensuring you get an accurately made garment. There are different ways to do this, but I have found these to be the most useful.

TAILOR'S TACKS
These can take a bit of time but are very useful on light delicate fabrics or ones that will mark easily.

1   Thread a needle, leaving the thread unknotted at the end. Sew a small stitch at the point that needs to be marked, but leave a small tail of thread.

2   Sew a second stitch but don't pull it tight; instead, leave it looped over the fabric and leave another tail before snipping off the thread (a).

3   Gently separate the layers of fabric and snip the threads between them. This will leave tails of threads in both layers of fabric to mark the points (b).

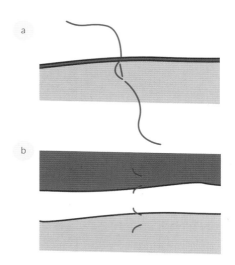

TAILOR'S CHALK AND MARKER PENS
Always keep the edges of traditional tailor's chalk slabs sharp so that you can use them to draw accurately. You can do this by pulling the edge of the chalk through a part-opened pair of old scissors, which shaves off some of the chalk, leaving a nice, fine edge – but make sure you do this over a bin.

Marker pens can be water soluble or just disappear on their own over time. They are great on plain or light-coloured fabrics, but they can get a bit lost on dark or highly patterned prints. Always remember to put the lid back on straight away, as they dry out very quickly.

To use either chalk or marker pens, make a small hole in the pattern piece at the points you wish to mark. Rub the chalk over the holes or lightly dab the marker pen through the holes and they will leave really accurate marks on your fabric.

PIN MARKING
This is a bit of a cheat, but it works in a similar way to tailor's tacks.

1   Place a pin in the pattern at the point to be marked and gently wiggle it though the paper.

2   Flip the fabric over. Where the pin is poking through the fabric, push another pin though to the pattern.

3   When the fabric is separated a pin should remain in each side of the fabric. Just be careful they don't fall out.

Interfacing

Interfacing is used to help support the fabric at key places such as a collar, neckline or waistline to help it keep its shape. It can be fusible or non-fusible and made from woven or non-woven fabric. Whichever type you use, it is fixed to the wrong side of the fabric.

I tend to use fusible (iron-on) interfacing, which has a rough texture on the wrong side due to the dots of adhesive. It's this rough side that needs to go against the wrong side of the fabric. Then you simply press the fabric with a steam iron: the heat and steam from the iron will melt the dots of glue and adhere the interfacing to the fabric.

I always place a pressing cloth between the iron and the fabric, just to make sure that the interfacing will not melt if the iron is too hot. This also protects the iron if the interfacing is the wrong way up and prevents it from getting stuck to the plate of the iron.

Darts

A dart is the simplest way to create shape. A basic dart is sewn from the edge of the pattern piece towards the fuller parts of the body, such as the bust, shoulder blades or buttocks.

1   Mark out the dart position on the fabric.

2   Fold the fabric with the right sides together, matching up the dart notches.

3   Sew from the notches in towards the point.

4   Secure your stitching the start and finish of your sewing. I like to reach the end of the dart and then drop my needle down and pivot so that I can sew back into the dart a little way.

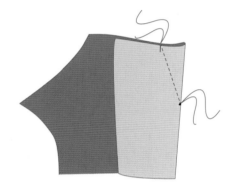

Simple seams

The easiest way to join two pieces of fabric is with a simple seam. You can then leave the seam as it is or neaten the raw edges if the seam will be visible. You don't need to neaten seams in a garment that is going to be lined.

1   Place the two pieces of fabric right sides together, matching up any notches or other pattern markings.

2   Position the fabric under the presser foot on the sewing machine so that the needle is sewing along the correct seam allowance. Drop the needle down about 1cm (⅜in) in from the back edge of the fabric.

3   Backstitch to the edge of the fabric, then sew forwards to the end of the seam. Stop and reverse about 1cm (⅜in) into your row of stitching.

4   Press the seam flat to set the stitches into the fabric.

You can then either press the seam to one side so that it is 'closed' or separate the two seam allowances and press the seam 'open' like a book.

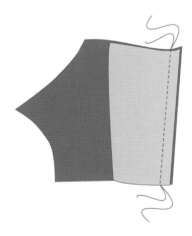

Reducing bulk

In order to reduce bulk and help the seam to lie flat, it sometimes needs to be trimmed down, usually by around half.

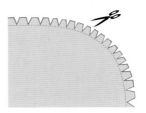

When sewing multiple layers of fabric in a seam, it's advisable to layer the seam allowances. This means trimming the layer of seam allowances down successively so they are graduated and will sit flat without creating a 'step'.

Curved seams need to be treated in a different way. The edges of the fabric will be a different length to the stitching line – think concentric circles. Snip into the seam allowance on a concave (or 'sad') curve at regular intervals to allow the seam to sit flat when folded back.

With a convex (or 'happy') curve, the edge of the fabric is longer than the stitching line so the seam allowance will pleat and bunch up, creating bulk when the seam allowance is folded back. Cut small V-shapes out of the seam allowance to enable it to sit nice and flat (see diagram).

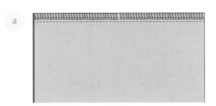

Neatening seams

OVERLOCKING (SERGING)

This is the quickest and easiest way to finish and neaten a seam. After sewing, overlock (serge) the seam trimming off just enough fabric to get a clean finish (a). Each side of a seam can be overlocked separately, but this is much trickier to do once the seam has been sewn, so most seams are finished closed.

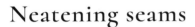

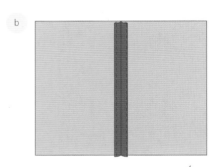

CLEAN FINISH

This is an excellent way to finish a seam if you do not possess an overlocker and are using a fairly lightweight fabric.

1   Stitch the seam, then press it open. Press under the raw edge of one seam allowance by 5mm (a scant ¼in).

2   Edge stitch the fold to hold it in place (b).

3   Repeat for the other side of the seam allowance.

MOCK OVERLOCK

This is just an elaborate zigzag stitch. Most modern sewing machines have a function for this and it gives the impression of an overlock but without cutting the fabric (c). You can achieve a similar finish with a simple zigzag stitch, but it is best to practise on some spare fabric to see which method works best with the fabric you are using.

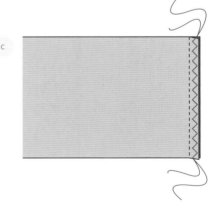

Machine stitching

EASE STITCHING

This is a single row of long machined stitches that can help one piece of fabric to fit into another – most commonly sewn over a set-in sleeve head to help it fit into the armhole (a). Ease stitching is similar to gathering stitches but you want to avoid any wrinkles or pleats in the fabric over the stitching line.

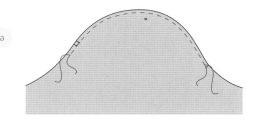

EDGE STITCHING

This is a visible row of stitches sewn very close to the edge of a seam or a section of a garment such as a collar (b). It is often confused with topstitching – but whereas topstitching can be anywhere on a garment, edge stitching is always on the edge.

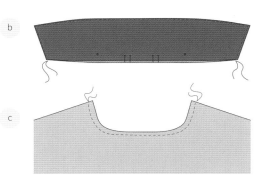

STAY STITCHING

This is a row of sewing inside the seam allowance, using the same or a slightly shorter stitch length than normal. It is usually done around a curve, such as a neckline, to help hold the fabric in the correct position as the garment is being made (c).

TOPSTITCHING

This can be just a single row or lots of rows of sewing that are visible from the right side of the fabric and used to highlight seams or areas of a garment such as pockets or collars for decoration (d).

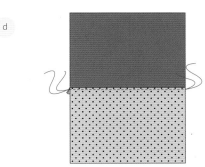

UNDERSTITCHING

Understitching helps to keep a facing or the underneath part of a garment rolled under. This is a row of sewing stitched through a facing and the seam allowance. Sew from the right side about 2mm (⅛in) away from the seam line to make sure that none of the main garment is caught.

GATHERS

Gathers are a great way of adding fullness to a garment.

1   Sew two or more rows of long stitches in parallel lines, within the seam allowance so they are not visible when the seams are sewn, leaving long tails of thread at the start and finish of each row (e).

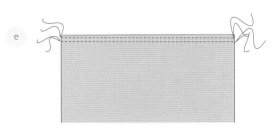

2   Gently pull the bobbin threads so that the fabric is ruched up along these threads.

3   When the fabric is gathered up to the required length, secure the threads by winding them around a pin in a figure of eight.

4   Spread the gathers out so that they are nice and even. Pin and sew them in place (f).

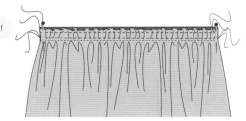

Buttonholes and buttons

SEWING A BUTTONHOLE

Marking up a buttonhole just takes a bit of patience and careful measuring.

1   Begin by positioning the top and bottom buttons. Now measure the distance between them and divide by the number of gaps between the buttons – so if you have six buttons, divide the total distance by five gaps.

2   Measure out each gap and mark it with a pin (a), chalk or a marker pen. This will give you the levels for each buttonhole.

3   To make sure the garment closes accurately along the centre lines, a vertical buttonhole needs to sit on that line, while a horizontal buttonhole needs to start just in front of it. The button will always pull to the furthest part of the buttonhole, so the end of the buttonhole needs to be just in front of the centre line. Mark this point on the fabric.

4   Carefully measure the distance from the edge of the fabric to the start of the buttonhole. Make sure each buttonhole is exactly the same so that your garment closure will be perfectly neat (b).

5   Most modern sewing machines have an automatic or semi-automatic buttonhole stitch, so use this to sew the buttonhole. If you have a buttonhole foot, drop the button into the back of the foot to gauge the length of the buttonhole. When you've stitched your buttonholes, carefully open them by slicing through the centre with a seam ripper or small sharp scissors. If you are using a seam ripper, place a pin across the end of the buttonhole so that you don't slice through the end.

SEWING ON A BUTTON

1   Overlap the two sides so that the centre lines are on top of each other. Make sure the top and bottom are level. Poke a pin, or mark with chalk or a marker pen through each open buttonhole.

2   Open the garment and note where the marks are; this will give you the button level. Re-mark each button position so that it lies along the centre line.

3   To sew on the button use a double thread and thread it through the eye of the needle so you have four threads. Knot the ends.

4   Sew a small stitch over the button position, then sew a second stitch and loop the thread over the needle to secure it. Trim off the tail of thread close to the fabric.

5   Pass the needle up through the eyes of the button and back down again into the fabric (c). Repeat this for 4–5 stitches to attach the button (d).

6   Bring the needle through the fabric underneath the button. Wrap the thread around the stitches between the button and fabric to hold the button away slightly. Pass the needle back to the wrong side of the garment and sew a small stitch through the back of the button position. Loop the thread over the needle and pull tight to secure the stitch. Cut off the thread close to the fabric.

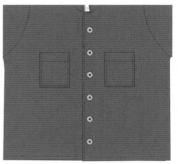

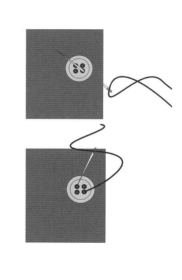

Using a twin needle

Sewing with a twin needle will require a second needle thread. The twin needle itself has a single shaft that's inserted into the needle holder block, but it also has a shoulder bar with two separate needles. They come in different sizes, like normal needles, and with different widths between the needles. Double check that you have the appropriate needle for the fabric you're working with.

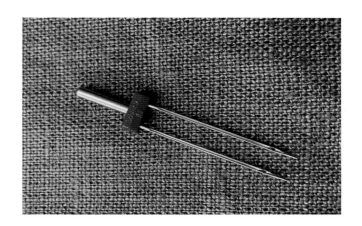

1   Some machines come with an extra spool holder, so use that if you have one. If not, pop the extra thread spool in a cup behind the sewing machine so that it can unwind freely.

2   Take both threads and pass them through the tension mechanism on the sewing machine together, as one. When it gets to the needle block, separate the threads and pass one through the right needle and one through the left.

3   Increase the stitch length to about 3.5–4, as this will be a topstitch and needs to float over the surface of the fabric. You may need to reduce the tension slightly to prevent a ridge from forming between the two lines of stitching. Always test the stitching on scraps of fabric first and note the setting for the fabric you use for future reference.

Double hem

A double hem will give a neat and solid finish to a hem.

1   Press up 1cm (⅜in) along the hem edge (a). Now fold that up again by the required hem depth and pin in place. Measure carefully to ensure a level hem.

2   Edge stitch along the folded top edge of the hem with a sewing machine or slipstitch by hand to hold the hem in place (b).

3   Give the hem a gentle steam and press to finish it.

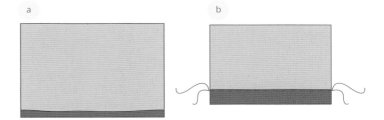

Pin hem

A pin hem gives a neat edge for fine, lightweight fabrics.

1   Fold and press up 1cm (⅜in) along the hem edge.

2   Sew 2mm (⅛in) from the folded edge around the hem (c).

3   Carefully trim back the hem allowance close to the row of sewing.

4   Fold up the trimmed hem again and sew directly on top of the first row of sewing (d).

5   Give the hem a gentle steam and press to finish the hem.

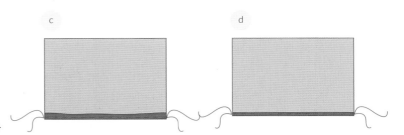

Hand sewing

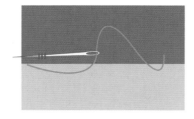

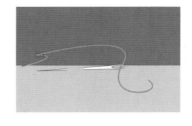

HERRINGBONE STITCH

The way the thread crosses over itself as the stitch is sewn creates a bit of stretch in the stitch and allows the fabric to move within it. It works well on both a double hem and a single layer, as it holds the hem flat to the garment.

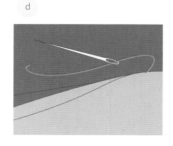

1   Working from left to right, anchor the thread into the hem. With the needle pointing to the left (or to the right if you are left handed and working from right to left), catch a few threads of the garment just above the hem. Keep the stitch as small and neat as you can (a).

2   Move the needle over to the right (left) by 1cm (⅜in), with the needle pointing to the left (right) again. Catch up a small bit of the hem fold (b).

3   Repeat these steps until you reach the end of the hem, then fasten off your stitching (c).

SLIPSTITCH

This works really well with a double hem, as most of the stitches are hidden under the hem.

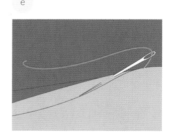

1   Working from right to left (or from left to right if you are left handed), anchor the thread into the hem (d).

2   Slip the needle through the fold of the hem for about 1cm (⅜in). As the needle comes back up, catch a few threads from the garment and pull the threads through to create the stitch (e).

3   Repeat all the way along the hem.

Basic embroidery stitches

There are many, many different embroidery stitches. I've used only these four in this book, but if you find that you enjoy embroidery there are plenty of tutorials available online.

FRENCH KNOTS

These can be used very effectively on their own or in groups. They can be spaced out to create a loose texture or when sewn densely together create a lovely raised surface. Great for adding texture and depth to a piece of embroidery.

1   Bring the needle up where you want the knot (a).

2   Wrap the thread 3 or 4 times around the needle (b and c).

3   Pull the thread fairly taut (d).

4   Push the needle back down into the fabric a few threads away from where it came out (e). This will anchor the knot in place (f) and you can move on to the next one.

STEM STITCH

Diagonally sewn stitches create a defined line of sewing and are a simple way of outlining a particular shape or creating flower or plant stems.

1   Bring the needle up at the start of the line you are going to follow (g).

2   Create the first stitch about 3mm (⅛in) long by bringing the needle back down diagonally. Make sure that the thread remains below the needle at all times (h).

3   Push the needle back out of the fabric above and just in front of the first stitch (i).

4   Make the second stitch by pushing the needle back down again diagonally, level but just in front of the first stitch (j).

5   Create the third stitch in the same way (k). Continue so you are sewing a diagonal row of stitches that are level at the top and bottom (l).

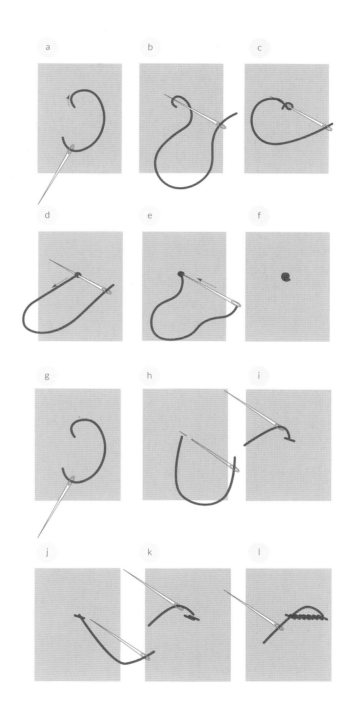

LONG AND SHORT STITCH

This is a wonderful way of filling in shapes and also blending colours. It combines both long and short stitches in an irregular pattern to start with, then a second color kind of fills in the gaps. It's a lovely way of 'painting with stitches'.

1   Bring your needle up at one end of your shape (a).

2   After deciding on the direction of the stitching, work your first long stitch about two-thirds of the way across the shape (b).

3   Work the second stitch directly next to the first, but make it shorter (c).

4   Work the third stitch directly next to the second one, but make it a different length again (d).

5   Continue to create stitches next to each other, but vary the stitch lengths to create an irregular pattern (e).

6   With a second colour thread bring up the needle at the end of the first stitch splitting the threads (f).

7   Fill in the gaps in the same way by creating stitches directly next to each other that meet the first colour stitches.

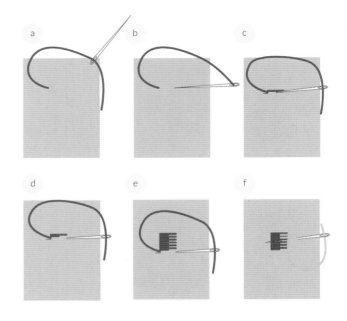

BLANKET STITCH

This is a lovely and decorative way to neaten off an edge.

1   Bring the needle up from the back of the fabric to the front at the beginning of the line of sewing (g).

2   Take the needle down through the fabric at the top of the first stitch. Bring the tip of the needle up in a direct vertical line down from where you inserted it (h), and a short distance along the sewing line; don't pull it through yet.

3   Place the working thread behind the needle; pull the needle through, creating a reverse L (i).

4   Continue stitching in the same manner, spacing the stitches at regular intervals and keeping them uniform in size (j and k), until you reach the end of your line (l).

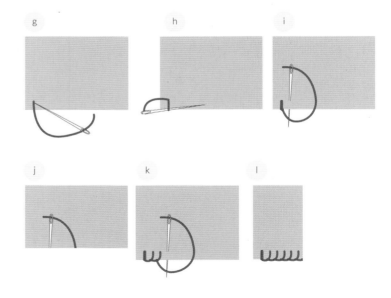

Sewing terms

Bias This is the diagonal grain of the fabric and it allows for more movement and drape of the material. Pattern pieces can be cut out on the bias to allow for a little stretch in the garment. Strips of fabric can be cut on the bias so that they will ease around curves.

Casing This is a double layer of fabric stitched to create a channel through which you can thread elastic or cord.

Facing A piece, or pieces, of fabric that usually mirror the opening to which they are attached. Facings are sewn around garment openings such as necklines or waistlines to neaten off and finish the raw edges.

Fold line Some pattern pieces are symmetrical so it is easier to cut just half the piece along the fold of a double-dover piece of fabric. This means no centre seam is required.

Finishing a seam Also referred to as 'neatening' a seam, this is just a way of preventing the raw edges of the fabric from fraying. You can use an overlocker (serger) or different stitches on a sewing machine, depending on the type of fabric you are working with.

Grain line The straight of grain is the direction of the warp thread on the fabric; it runs parallel to the selvedges. The grain line on your pattern is a long line with an arrow at each end. Aligning the pattern grain line with the straight of grain on your fabric will ensure that your garment hangs straight and true.

Layering This is when one side of the seam allowance is trimmed back further than the other to create a 'stepped' effect. It reduces bulk.

Notch Sometimes referred to as balance marks, notches allow you to match up pattern pieces together accurately when you are making up a garment.

Selvedge This is the neat edge that runs along both long edges of the fabric. It is created when the horizontal weft threads in the fabric, which are woven over and under the vertical warp thread, get to the end and then turn back on themselves and are woven in the other way. It has very little 'give' and allows the fabric to hang 'true' and straight.

Tacking (basting) A temporary row of long stitches to hold the fabric in place until it is stitched permanently.

Templates

Templates shown at 50%

You can download printable
versions of these templates from:
www.davidandcharles.com

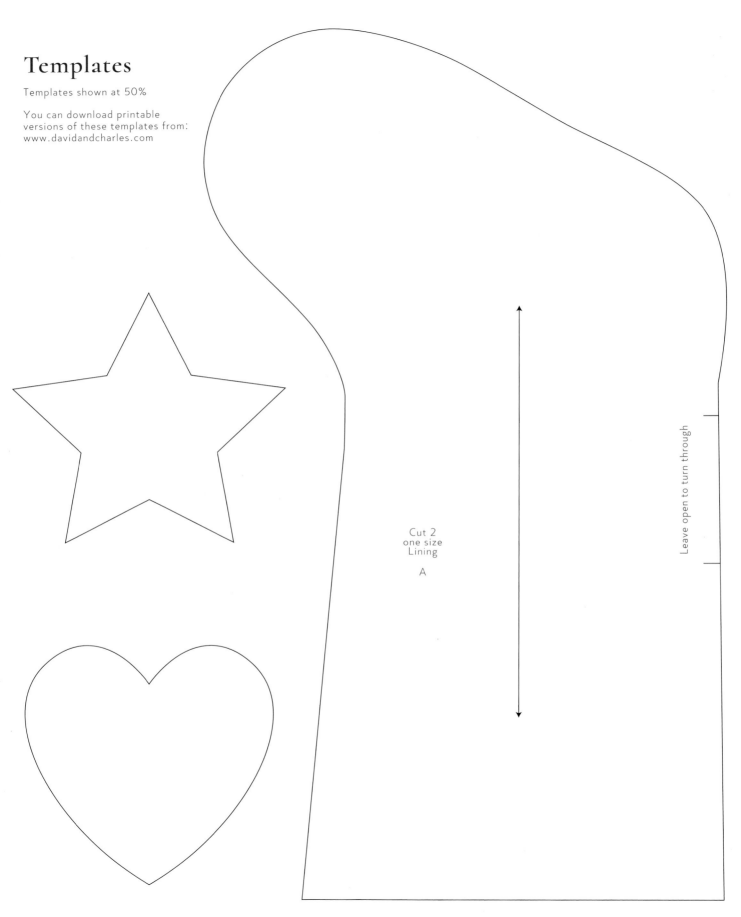

Cut 2
one size
Lining

A

Leave open to turn through

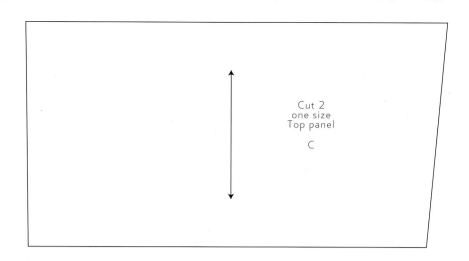

Cut 2
one size
Top panel

C

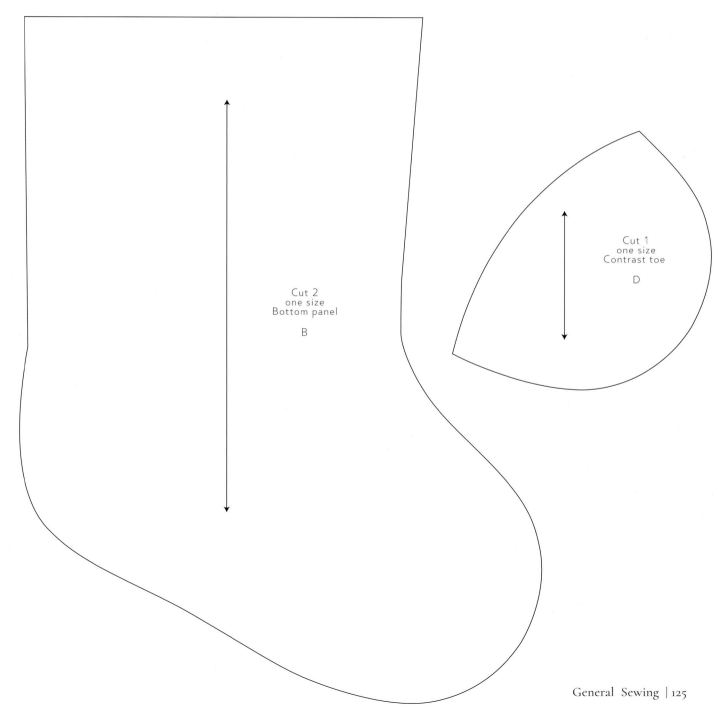

Cut 2
one size
Bottom panel

B

Cut 1
one size
Contrast toe

D

About the Author

Jules Fallon has been sewing for as long as she can remember. Having been a professional designer and pattern cutter in the fashion industry for over 10 years, Jules fell into teaching when her children were small. She lectured in Fashion and Design for almost 10 years until she started Sew Me Something, her multi-award-winning studio and haberdashery. Using her professional training Jules now runs sewing and craft workshops and retreats from her studio in Stratford upon Avon, as well as designing and producing her own range of dressmaking patterns, all of which are available at www.sewmesomething.co.uk.

Acknowledgements

I would like to thank my husband Charlie and the SMS team for allowing me the freedom to just get my head down and write this book, leaving them to deal with everything else. I'd also like to thank the team at David and Charles for their editing support and keeping me to the deadlines, something I'm not usually very good at. Thanks also go to Laura Staddon from The Craft Cakery (www.thecraftcakery.com) who made all the delicious-looking cakes in the book.

Index

Apple Cake, Spiced Sugar Crust 84–7
appliqué 107
autumn, project ideas for 65–87

belts 23
bias strips 27–8
bias tape, iron-on 77
binding 27–9
Blanket, Reloved 80–3
blanket stitch 83, 122
brocade 104
bulk reduction 116
buttonholes 23, 47, 70, 73, 97, 102, 118
buttons 16, 23, 47, 70, 73, 97, 118

cakes
    Chocolate Orange 34–7
    Lemon Drizzle 60–3w
    Rich Fruit 108–11
    Spiced Sugar Crust Apple 84–7
Cami and Shorts 54–9
Chocolate Orange Cake 34–7
Christmas Stocking 104–7, 124–5
Cider Nog, Hot 85, 87
Coat, Winter 90–7
collars 21–2, 69–70, 93, 95–6
Cordial, Elderflower 61–3
cotton 11, 24, 48, 54, 98, 104
Curd, Orange 36–7
cutting out 8, 114

darts 12, 20, 93, 97, 114, 115
denim 16, 66
Drawstring Trousers 98–103
Dress, Shirt 16–23

ease stitching 117
edge stitching 117
elastic 11, 51, 53, 59, 102
Elderflower Cordial 61–3
embroidery
    Embroidered Tee 30–3
    embroidery hoops 32
    stitches 121–2
equipment 8–9

fabrics 11
    see also specific types of fabric
facings 21–2, 69–72, 93, 95–6
fly zips 43–4
French knots 121
Fruit Cake, Rich 108–11

Ganache, Chocolate 36–7
gathers 117

haberdashery 11
hand sewing 120–2
hems 73, 79
    double 119, 120
    pin 119
herringbone stitch 120

interfacing 11, 18–19, 42, 68–9, 92–3, 115
ironing 8–9

jersey fabric 74–9

knit fabric 11, 74, 80–3

Latte, Homemade Mocha 34–7
lay plans 13
Lemon Drizzle Cake 60–3
linen 11, 16, 24, 40, 66, 98
linings, coat 97
long stitch 122

machine stitching 117
marking patterns 114
mock overlock 116
Mulled Wine 109, 111

needles 8
    twin 119
Nog, Hot Cider 85, 87

Orange Curd 36–7
overlocking (serging) 8, 74, 116

Palazzo Pants 40–7
patterns 12
    drafting 26
    transferring 114
pins 8
    pin marking 114
plackets 69–70
pockets 16, 19, 45, 69–70, 94, 101

ribbon 107

seams
    bulk reduction 116
    neatening 116
    side 45, 94
    simple 115

sewing machines 8
sewing techniques 113–23
sewing terminology 123
Shirred Summer Top 48–53
shirts
    Oversized Shirt 66–73
    Shirt Dress 16–23
short stitch 122
Shorts and Cami 54–9
silk 54
sizing 12
sleeves 21, 72–3, 78–9, 96
slipstitch 120
spring, project ideas for 15–37
stay stitching 117
stem stitch 121
straps, camisole 57–8
summer, project ideas for 39–63

T-shirt, Classic 74–9
tabs 72–3
tailor's chalk/tacks 114
Tees
    Embroidered 30–3
    Woven 24–9
thread 11
tools 8–9
top stitching 117
tops
    Shirred Summer Top 48–53
    see also shirts; T-shirt; Tee
transferring pattern markings 114
trousers
    Drawstring Trousers 98–103
    Palazzo Pants 40–7

understitching 117

velvet 104
viscose 11, 40, 48

waistbands 46–7, 102–3
Wine, Mulled 109, 111
winter, project ideas for 89–111
wool 11, 90–7
woven fabrics 11, 24–9

yokes 69, 70–2

zips 11, 43–4

A DAVID AND CHARLES BOOK
© David and Charles, Ltd 2021

David and Charles is an imprint of David and Charles, Ltd
Suite A, Tourism House, Pynes Hill, Exeter, EX2 5WS

Text and Designs © Jules Fallon 2021
Layout and Photography © David and Charles, Ltd 2021

First published in the UK and USA in 2021

A catalogue record for this book is available from the British Library.

ISBN-13: 9781446308745 paperback
ISBN-13: 9781446380840 EPUB

This book has been printed on paper from approved suppliers and made from pulp from sustainable sources.

Printed in China by Asia Pacific for:
David and Charles, Ltd
Suite A, Tourism House, Pynes Hill, Exeter, EX2 5WS

10 9 8 7 6 5 4 3 2 1

Senior Commissioning Editor: Sarah Callard
Editor: Jessica Cropper
Project Editor: Sarah Hoggett
Head of Design: Sam Staddon
Photography: Jason Jenkins
Art Direction and Layout: Laura Woussen
Pre-press Designer: Ali Stark
Illustrations: Jules Fallon
Production Manager: Beverley Richardson

David and Charles publishes high-quality books on a wide range of subjects. For more information visit www.davidandcharles.com.

Layout of the digital edition of this book may vary depending on reader hardware and display settings.